SCORE!

Super Closers, Openers, Revisiters, Energizers

BY

Becky Pike
Pluth, M.Ed., CSP

Rich Meiss, MBA

Karen Carlson

Scott Enebo, M.A.

Janice Horne

Ayako Nakamura

Bob Pike, CSP, CPAE

Jaime Pylant

Marc Ratcliffe, M.Ed.

Adrianne Roggenbuck, M.Ed.

Priscilla Shumway, M.Ed.

Enhanced Results for Face to Face Training

☐ ☐ ☐ SCORE! SUPER CLOSERS, OPENERS, REVIEWS, ENERGIZERS, VOLUME 3

by
Becky Pike Pluth, M.ED., CSP
Rich Meiss, MBA
Karen Carlson
Scott Enebo, M.A.
Janice Horne
Ayako Nakamura
Bob Pike, CSP, CPAE
Jaime Pylant
Marc Ratcliffe, M.ED.
Adrianne Roggenbuck, M.ED.
Priscilla Shumway, M.ED.

Cover Design by Majeres Graphic Design
Internal Layout by Alan Pranke
Compiled and Edited by Rich Meiss
Copy Editing and Proof Reading by Liz Wheeler
Edited by Liz Wheeler
©2013 Creative Training Techniques Productions LLC

Text copyright: Becky Pike Pluth, Rich Meiss, Karen Carlson, Scott Enebo, Janice Horne, Ayako Nakamura, Bob Pike, Jaime Pylant, Marc Ratcliffe, Adrianne Roggenbuck and Priscilla Shumway.

ALL RIGHTS RESERVED

Permission is granted by the authors for the purchaser of this book to copy and use designated pages only in seminars and meetings. Unless specifically designated, no part of this publication may be reproduced, stored in a retrieval system, or transmitted in any form or by any means, electronic, mechanical, photocopy, scanning or otherwise except as permitted under the United States 1976 Copyright Act or by written permission from the publisher.

ISBN: 978-0-9896615-0-8

10 9 8 7 6 5 4 3 2 1

Printed in the United States of America

Publisher
Creative Training Techniques Productions LLC
14530 Martin Drive
Eden Prairie MN 55344

For additional books or quantity discounts, contact:
The Bob Pike Group
Phone: 800-383-9210 and 952-829-1954
Fax: 952-829-0260
Email: csheffield@bobpikegroup.com

THANK YOU TO MENTORS, COLLEAGUES AND CLIENTS

We thank our many mentors, colleagues and clients with whom we've had the privilege of working throughout our careers in the training and human resource development field. You have sharpened our minds and helped us develop many of the concepts which we now teach.

Thank you to the tens of thousands of presenters, trainers and facilitators with whom we've worked over the last 30+ years. Many of you have given us great ideas, and/or allowed us to try out these ideas in your sessions. We appreciate the chance to work with so many great people, and would also welcome any feedback on the exercises in this book.*

We extend a special thank you to the training consultants of The Bob Pike Group. Karen, Scott, Janice, Ayako, Bob, Jaime, Marc, Adrianne, and Priscilla — you bring a professionalism and passion to your training that makes it a joy to work together. Thank you for your commitment to participant-centered training and for your creativity in putting together these exercises.

Thank you to Jody Majeres, Alan Pranke and Liz Wheeler for your graphic design and editing skills.

And a special thanks to the loves of our lives, Brad Pluth and Barbara Meiss, for your encouragement and continued support of projects like these.

Becky Pike Pluth and Rich Meiss

I'd like to extend a very special thank you to Rich Meiss for creating the SCORE! brand with our dear friend Doug McCallum and for his tireless work on this project.

Becky Pike Pluth

*See *"Your Name in Lights"* on page 131 for a way to contribute your own activity to another version of this book.

CONTENTS

Introduction 7
How to Use this Book 9
Closers 11
    At the Cafeteria 13
    Be a Palm Reader 15
    Celebration Card Closer 17
    Choose or Lose 18
    Handy Information 21
    Kinesthetic Evaluation 23
    $100 Bill 25
    One Minute Summary 27
    Piece of Pie 29
    Six-Word Story 30
    S.M.A.S.H. and Grab! 32
    Spies and Allies 34
Openers 37
    Appointment Calendar Clock 38
    Chocolate Personalities 40
    Clinch the Cliché 43
    Icon-Ku 44
    Learning Mascot 46
    Mirror Image 48
    Paper Balancing 50
    Robbed Museum 53
    Standards and Norms 55
    Superhero Sorting 56
    T Puzzle 58
    We're a Puzzle, but Still a Team 61
    Which is More Important? 63
    Which Words? 64

Revisiters 67
Board Game Re-Do 69
Card Questions 70
Confounded 72
Create a Mural 75
Dice of Fate 77
Myth Buster 79
Playing Card Questions 81
Safari Wall 82
Shape Friends 85
Survey Says 87
Turn the Cards 88
Up and At 'Em 90

Energizers 93
Back to Back Counting 95
Board Meeting 96
Cross Lateral Stretch 99
Fancy Feet 101
Getting to the Point 103
Great Generational Truths 104
How You Doin'? 106
John Hancock 109
Need Caffeine? 110
Sniglets 112
State Land Mammals 116
Superheroes 120
Top 10 Energy Drink Consumers 122
Usual Suspects 124
What do They Stand for? 126

Your Name in Lights 131
About the Authors 133

INTRODUCTION

This is the first book of the SCORE! series to be published since my daughter, Becky Pike Pluth, took the helm of The Bob Pike Group. Her theme for this first year is collaboration – and she demonstrates it clearly in this volume.

Becky has worked with our trainers to gather a powerful collection of activities that serve as frames for the content of almost any training program. There is a wonderful balance between closers, openers, revisiters and energizers. Whether your class is an hour or several weeks, you'll find activities that you can modify to fit your time requirements.

As with previous volumes, remember the three As – Adapt, Adopt, Apply. And be sure to take advantage of the videos connected to the QR codes that help you gain a better understanding of many of the activities – another first for this book series.

For those not familiar with The Bob Pike Group or Creative Training Techniques™, it will help to remember that our focus is on instructor-led, but participant-centered training. Thousands of corporate trainers on five continents have been through BPG's "Train the Trainer Boot Camp." The focus is always on inspiring, empowering, and equipping participants to get better results both professionally and personally. And that is what the activities in this volume are designed to help you as a trainer or instructional designer do – to more fully engage your learners so they learn faster, better, easier – and then transfer the new knowledge and skills into results back on the job!

So pick an activity, try it out, and then add more into your training or your designs. I know that Becky will always welcome your feedback – as well as any ideas you may have for future volumes of SCORE!

Bob Pike CSP, CPAE, MPCT, CPLP Fellow

Founder and Chairman Emeritus, The Bob Pike Group

HOW TO USE THIS BOOK

Here are four simple steps for using this book effectively:

1. Remind yourself why it is important to use closers, openers, revisiters and energizers by reading the first page of each chapter.

2. Select the appropriate category – closers, openers, revisiters or energizers.

3. Pick the best exercise for your content and purpose.

4. Practice, practice and practice the exercise before you actually use it.

Why use Closers, Openers, Revisiters and Energizers?

Each chapter gives more detail about the reasons to use these CORE exercises in your presentations, but here is a general overview.

Too many presentations simply start and end without a process or purpose. Yet research reveals that people remember best what they see or hear first and last, so we need to start strong and end strong – using good openers and closers. The purpose of revisiters is to make sure the participants really learn the content. A favorite phrase we use is "just because you said it doesn't mean they learned it." Review multiple times with a variety of methods to ensure learning takes place. And energizers are used to keep participants alive in the session.

What Categories Are Included in the Book?

Although many of these exercises can be used for multiple purposes, we have divided them into four key categories, with energizers having two subcategories:

Closers

Openers

Revisiters

Energizers

They are the CORE to help you SCORE and win in your presentations. Each exercise has been placed into one of these categories and put in that section of the book. In addition, we have often indicated that the exercise may be used for another purpose. For example, several of the revisiter techniques are also good energizers.

HOW TO USE THIS BOOK

How Do I Decide Which Exercise to Use?

There are many details to consider before choosing an exercise. What is my purpose? What do I know about my audience, and will this exercise work for them? What about time and space considerations? What materials do I need, and how much will it cost to purchase them? Will participants be able to gain a learning point and apply it as a result of the exercise? You can answer these questions briefly by glancing at the format of each page.

Why Do I Need to Practice the Exercise?

Good presenters make an exercise look easy, but usually that is only because they have used it a number of times. Our experience is that we need to try out an exercise several times — either on some friends and relatives in a low-risk setting or in front of a mirror by ourselves — before we have the word track and the flow down to use it effectively. Remember the six Ps: Proper Preparation and Practice Prevent Poor Performance!

Enjoy these CORE exercises!

SCORE III: SUPER CLOSERS, OPENERS, REVISITERS AND ENERGIZERS

CLOSERS

For many years we've taught presenters, trainers and facilitators the value of closing their sessions with power. Along with openings, closings are the most valuable real estate that a presenter has as they form the bookends to the presentation. They should set the stage for the session and close it with impact. Too often we hear sessions close with, *"I see our time is up. We'll see you next time!"* or *"Be sure to complete your evaluation on the way out."*

These are not effective closings! Make sure that you have a closing **ACT**. This includes **A**ction planning, **C**elebration, and **T**ying things together:

A – Action planning, goal setting or reflection time: Give the participants some time to reflect on the important concepts or ideas learned in the session. What are they going to do with the information? How are they going to apply it? By spending some time reflecting and writing, there is a much greater chance that they will both retain more of the information and actually apply it. Unfortunately the opposite is also true. If participants have no time to reflect on the content and think about its application in the program, they probably will have no time to apply their new learning when they return to their jobs.

C – Celebration: Usually participants have invested time, energy, maybe even money, in attending your presentation. They have probably learned new things. Maybe they have gained new skills. They've made difficult decisions or solved tough problems. They leave having provided useful input. All of these are reasons to celebrate their investment! Celebration can take many forms. It might be something formal such as certificates of completion given out at a training event, or it might be a more informal celebration – the awarding of small prizes, congratulations from the boss, or even just a quick high-five among the group members for their accomplishment.

T – Tie things together: A great presentation comes full circle and ties the opening and closing together. In a meeting, for example, the agenda is introduced in the beginning and then quickly reviewed at the end. Training sessions circle back to the stated objectives to make sure participants are satisfied with the outcomes. An opening exercise is referred to again as the program is concluded. Then close with a powerful ending – a quote, story, question, or call to action.

Here are some great, proven closers for you to use.

http://bit.ly/SCORE3Closers

AT THE CAFETERIA ☐ ☐ ☐

Author: Ayako Nakamura

Description: Use this activity to help participants think about application of their learning on-the-job.

Objective: To clearly visualize what and how the participants would apply their learning on-the-job

Audience: Any training audience

Time: 5-10 minutes

Group Size: Any size, formed into groups of 2-3 people

Materials: None

Process:
1. Group the participants into pairs or trios. Tell them that they are going to see each other at the cafeteria three months from now and will recognize each other from this training.

2. Ask participants to start a conversation among themselves by someone saying: "Hi, how have you been? We were at the XYZ training program together awhile ago!" Then ask them what they applied from the training on-the-job and what the results were.

3. Take 5 minutes for them to have a conversation.

Debrief: Ask several participants to share their conversations and what they have been applying on the job.

BE A PALM READER

Author: Adrianne Roggenbuck

Description: This works best as a closer at the end of a session.

Objective: Recall three to five key ideas from the class and create an action plan.

Audience: Any training audience

Time: 10 minutes

Group Size: Any size will work as this is done individually first and then shared orally

Materials: Blank sheet of paper and writing instrument for each person

Process:
1. Have participants trace the outline of their hand on a sheet of paper.

2. Ask them to write down three to five key ideas that they would like to have "at their fingertips" following the class. Each key idea is written on a separate finger.

3. On the palm of their handprint, they will write their "action plan" of what they intend to do with this information when they return to work.

Debrief: Participants take their handprint with them and find a partner from another table with whom to talk. They will "read each other's palms" to share their Action Plans.

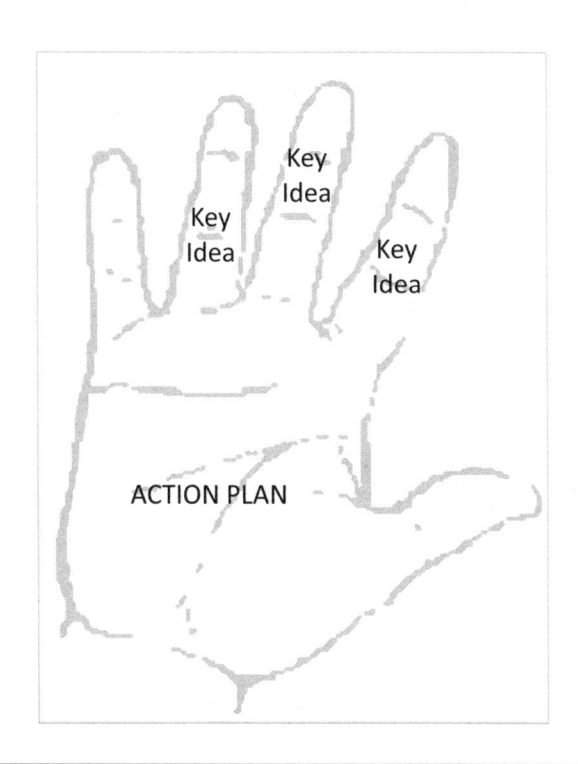

Super Closers, Openers, Revisiters, Energizers, Volume 3

CELEBRATION CARD CLOSER ☐ ☐ ☐

Author: Bob Pike

Description: This activity will reinforce the class learnings and allow for participant recognition

Objective: To identify action ideas and give recognition to co-participants

Audience: Any training audience

Time: 7-10 minutes

Group Size: Any size, split into subgroups of 5-7 people

Materials: 3"x5" card for each participant

Process:

1. Participants are each given a card and one minute to write their names on the front of the card and the single most important thing they've learned during the class and how they plan to use it.

2. After a minute, all the cards are passed to one person in the group. This person redistributes the cards so that no one at the table has his or her own card.

3. On the back of the card, each person has one minute to complete this sentence about the person who owns the card: One contribution that [name] has made to us during this training is _____.

4. After a minute, the person that distributed the cards starts the round robin process by saying: "I have [name's] card. Here's what he or she plans to do," and then reads aloud the sentence the person wrote on the front of the card. The reader then turns the card over and reads the praise sentence about the person. The reader then hands the card to its owner. The owner is only allowed to say, "Thank you."

5. Then the owner of that first card repeats the process with the card he or she received. This continues until everyone in the group has their own card back.

http://bit.ly/SCORE3CCC

Super Closers, Openers, Revisiters, Energizers, Volume 3

☐ ☐ ☐ CHOOSE OR LOSE

Author: Marc Ratcliffe

Description: This is a reflective closing activity that will provide some action after the training has concluded. The idea is to ask the participants to consider one or two key things they would like to implement after the program based on what they have learned (this is the "choose" part of the activity), as well as one or two things they would like to stop doing in their normal practice (this is the "lose" part).

Objective: Identify specific action items for participants to focus on post-training.

Audience: Any training audience

Time: 10-15 minutes

Group Size: Any size

Materials: Index cards and writing instruments

Process:
1. Provide each participant with a blank index card and ask them to write "Choose" on one side and "Lose" on the other side.

2. Next, encourage participants to add one or two points under each heading.

3. Once all participants have completed their cards, the trainer should organize them into teams of 3-6 people and ask them to share what was written on their index cards among their teams.

Debrief: The trainer should remind the participants that the transfer of concepts to their workplaces rests with them and, if they have the courage to try something new as well as to discontinue unproductive or inefficient practices, they are one step closer to improved performance. This "choose or lose" card is therefore the first step in creating the changes needed.

Variations:
1. Provide the audience with envelopes and ask them to self-address them. Finally, collect each of the index cards, attach stamps and post them on the participants' behalf about three weeks after the training. In this way, the card acts as both a closer to content as well as a reminder of the content post-training. There will be greater impact for the participants as they are essentially creating advice for themselves from themselves. The arrival of the envelope could also kick-start the implementation process if it hadn't already started.

2. Replace the index card with two different colored sticky notes and then present the "choose" or "lose" findings on the wall in a prominent location. This would be particularly useful for a longer program to support the on-going reflection of content.

3. This activity could be done in a similar way for online learning by replacing the index card with a virtual sticky and the small groups with a private online chat room for three to six people.

Choose

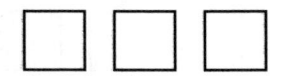

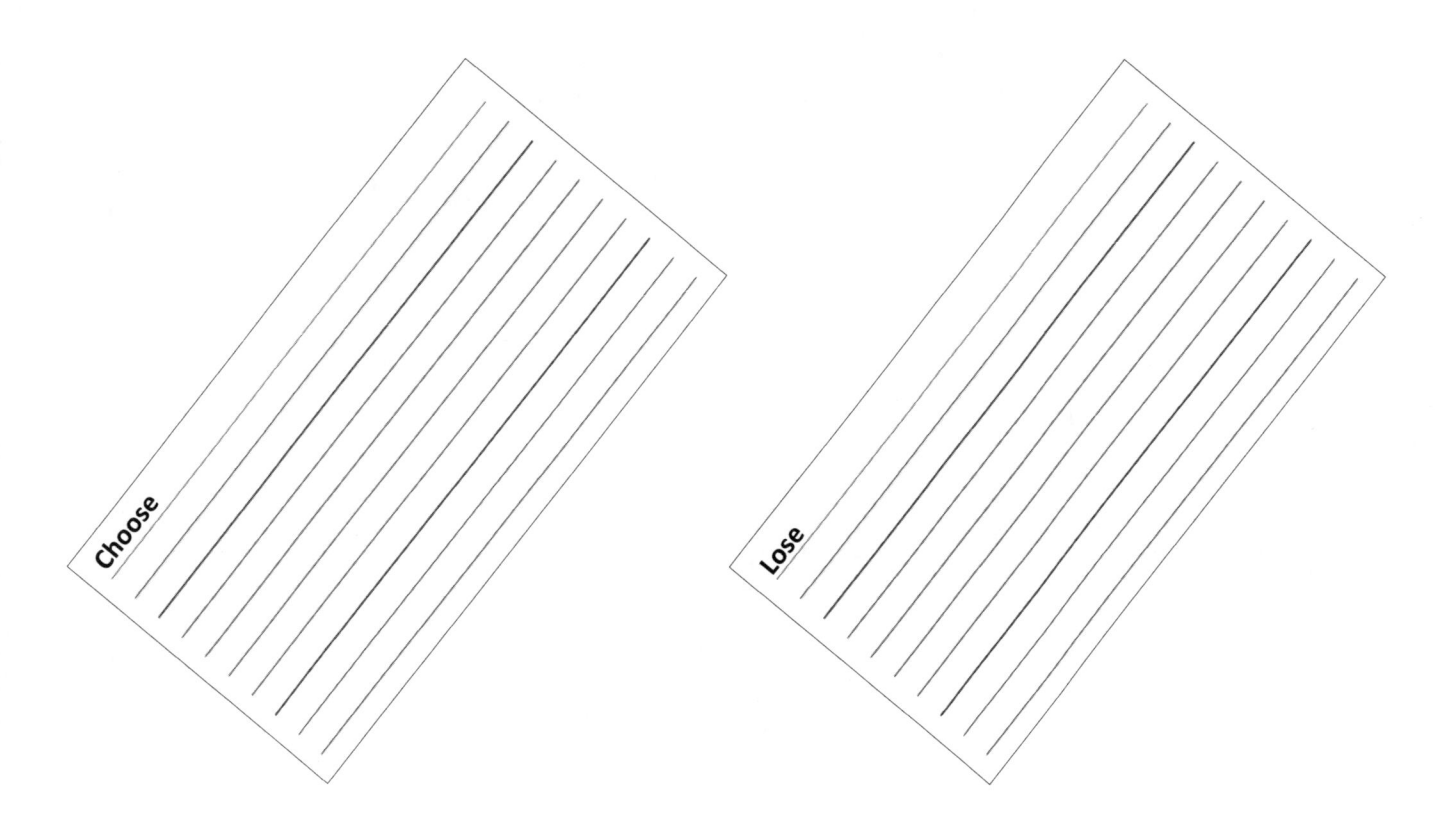

Lose

HANDY INFORMATION

Author: Priscilla Shumway

Description: This closer helps identify value gained in a training session.

Objective: To reflect and record key learning points from a training

Audience: Any training audience

Time: 5 minutes

Group Size: Any size

Materials: Blank paper, writing instrument

Process: Ask participants to trace one of their hands on a blank sheet of paper. Then label each finger with the following comments from the session:

>Thumb: What was something new that opposed what you already thought or did? (Opposable thumbs)

>Pointer finger: What was something new that was pointed out to you?

>Middle finger: What was the biggest new idea? (Middle fingers are usually the longest.)

>Ring finger: What was something that rings true? (Something you are already doing.)

>Pinky finger: What is one small change you can make that will make a difference?

Debrief: Depending on the size of the group, you can have them share with their team, a partner or the whole group.

Variations: To share with a new partner, find someone who has a similar hand size to you and share. Participants must stand up and match hands. If you are short on time, participants can chose three of the five fingers to write about.

KINESTHETIC EVALUATION

Author: Priscilla Shumway

Description: This is a short physical closing activity that is humorous and allows people to leave feeling very upbeat.

Objective: This activity signals the end of a session.

Audience: Any training or presentation audience

Time: 30 seconds

Group Size: Any size

Materials: None

Process:
1. Ask participants to:
   - Stand up.
   - Turn around in a circle.
   - Close your eyes; now open them.
   - Raise your right hand in a fist and tap the left part of your chest three times.
2. Say, "Now when someone asks you how the training session went you can say, 'It brought me to my feet, it turned me around, it opened my eyes and it touched my heart.'"

Variations: Share with a partner one thing that you picked up from the class that either opened your eyes or touched your heart.

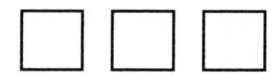

$100 BILL

Author: Priscilla Shumway

Description: This closer encourages participants to evaluate all of the material presented and prioritize how they will apply it. Participants must plan for using the material back on the job.

Objective: For participants to choose the most valuable thing they have learned from the class that they will implement within the next two weeks.

Audience: Any training audience

Time: 5 minutes

Group Size: Any size

Materials: Oversized copies of $100 bills either copied on a photocopier or purchased from various joke stores.

Process:
1. Hand out a copy of an oversized $100 bill to each participant.

2. Say, "I believe that it pays to come to training. On the back of your $100 bill, write what was the most VALUABLE thing you learned today. What was the one thing that was 'worth the price of admission'? What is one thing that an observer would be sure to see you doing differently back on the job as a result of this class?"

Debrief: Have learners turn to the person next to them or team up with their learning partner and share what they wrote on their bill.

Variations: Have participants write their names and phone numbers or email addresses on the bill and exchange them with a teammate. Each teammate is then responsible for contacting the other person in two weeks to follow up on how well the ideas were implemented.

Super Closers, Openers, Revisiters, Energizers, Volume 3

ONE MINUTE SUMMARY ☐ ☐ ☐

Author: Rich Meiss

Description: Have participants summarize the most important content from the seminar in one minute.

Objective: Challenge the participants to describe the most important learning from the seminar in one minute; provide focus on the topic and its key content pieces.

Audience: Any training audience

Time: 5-10 minutes

Group Size: Any size divided into subgroups of 4-6 people

Materials: Flip chart paper and markers for each table group (or piece of paper and pens at tables)

Process:
1. Have the participants work as a table group for this exercise.

2. Tell the group that they will have exactly 4 minutes to create a 1-minute summary for the class on the key point(s) from today's class. They can spend the entire time elaborating on one key point, or cover up to four key points, briefly touching on each. Tell them to chart out the key points to assist them in their presentations.

3. Allow 4 minutes to prepare and then have all groups report out to the entire group. Use a stopwatch to time each presentation.

Variations: Give a prize for the group that gets closest to 60 seconds in summarizing the content.

http://bit.ly/SCORE3POP

PIECE OF PIE ☐ ☐ ☐

Author: Scott Enebo

Description: This activity helps everyone identify the best thoughts and actionable ideas from the session in order to encourage action as participants get ready to leave at the end of a session.

Objective: To allow participants to reflect on the learning from the session and decide what is most relevant and important for implementation on the job.

Audience: Any training audience

Time: 10 minutes

Group Size: Any size

Materials: Piece of paper and writing instrument

Process:
1. Ask everyone to take out a piece of paper and a writing implement. Say, "Based on what we have talked about here today, I would like for you to answer the following questions."
2. Here is what they write. (Model this on a piece of chart paper.)
   A. P – Priceless piece of information. What has been the most important piece of information for you today?
   B. I – Item to implement. What is something you intend to implement from our time today?
   C. E – Encouragement I received. What is something that I am already doing that I was encouraged to keep on doing?

Debrief: Use the following situations and questions for debrief.
1. Turn to a partner and share what it is that you wrote down.
2. What were some of the key words that you heard while you shared?
3. What were the common themes that kept coming up?
4. What would it mean for our organization if we implemented the things on your papers?
5. What would it mean if we did NOT implement the things on your papers?
6. What are the next steps that you think we should take together?

Variations:
1. Instead of sharing with a partner, have everyone get in a circle and share one or more of the things that they wrote on their piece of paper.
2. Try and bring in some actual pie as you close the session. As you eat the pie, have people answer the questions above as well as talk about how the image or object of "pie" is relevant to the work that they are expected to do.

Super Closers, Openers, Revisiters, Energizers, Volume 3

☐ ☐ ☐ SIX-WORD STORY

Author: Scott Enebo

Description: This concept has history that traces back to Ernest Hemingway. Legend says that Ernest Hemingway once won a bet that he could write a six-word story that could make people cry. This challenge is a test to help participants distill their learning into six short words to get at the true essence of what they are taking away.

Objective: To encourage participants to distill their wisdom into six words and get at a key learning from the training session.

Audience: Any training audience

Time: 5-10 minutes

Group Size: Any size

Materials: Paper, writing instrument

Process:
1. Say, "There is a legend that Ernest Hemingway once won a bet by writing a six-word story that was so good that it made people cry. While I do not intend for us to cry at the end of this (unless you want to), I am going to challenge each of you to write a six-word story that captures the most important learning for you today. Try and make it as complete as possible but still allow for interpretation as people think about the words that you select."
2. Clarify instructions.
3. Allow time to write.
4. Go around the room and let people share their six-word stories.

Debrief: This may not require a debrief as the participants' words are intended to be the closing ideas for a session or a piece of content before break. If you care to debrief, here are a few ideas:
1. What words jumped out at you?
2. What comments do you remember?
3. What was the challenge in writing this?
4. What made it easy to get these words on the page?
5. What stories had an impact on you?
6. Are there barriers to having your story play out the way you'd like? What are they?
7. What would be the impact if your story were implemented at work?

30 SCORE! III

Variations: Make this a carryover activity where you ask everyone to turn in their six-word stories. In 30 days, you can send a reminder to learners about the stories they wrote for themselves and see how they are doing in making that story come to life. This will give great anecdotal evidence of the training as well as be a powerful reminder of the training itself.

http://bit.ly/SCORE36WS

☐ ☐ ☐ S.M.A.S.H. AND GRAB!

Author: Marc Ratcliffe

Description: This closing activity delves more deeply and encourages reflection by asking five questions. Each question begins with one of the letters in the word "SMASH."

Objective: Identify key items to follow-up and actions to be taken by participants post-training.

Audience: Any training audience

Time: 5-10 minutes

Group Size: Any size

Materials: Notepad, writing instruments

Process: Ask the participants to reflect upon their learning by responding to the following questions on their notepads.

As a result of the training, what will you:

- **S**tart Doing?
- **M**odify?
- **A**ct Upon?
- **S**top Doing?
- **H**elp someone with?

Alternatively, the trainer could have prepared cards with the letters S, M, A, S, and H printed downwards on the left hand side of the card, leaving enough room for a response next to each letter.

Once the participants have reflected on each of the items, ask them to share with others in the room. This is the "grab" part of the activity.

Debrief: In the debrief, the trainer could ask the following:

1. Why would we want you to consider more than just takeaways?
2. Why would we have you consider things to start and stop doing?
3. What is the importance of considering modifications and things to help others with?

Variations: 1. This activity could be done collaboratively as a small group where they discuss the five options and negotiate combined answers for each. This could then be shared verbally group by group or graphically via a poster.

2. This could be set up as an ongoing activity with SMASH posters arranged around the training room. Participants would be asked to place relevant responses to the propositions whenever they had something to add. The trainer could encourage the participants to review each of the posters as a final closer and "grab" any new ideas that they would like to implement for themselves.

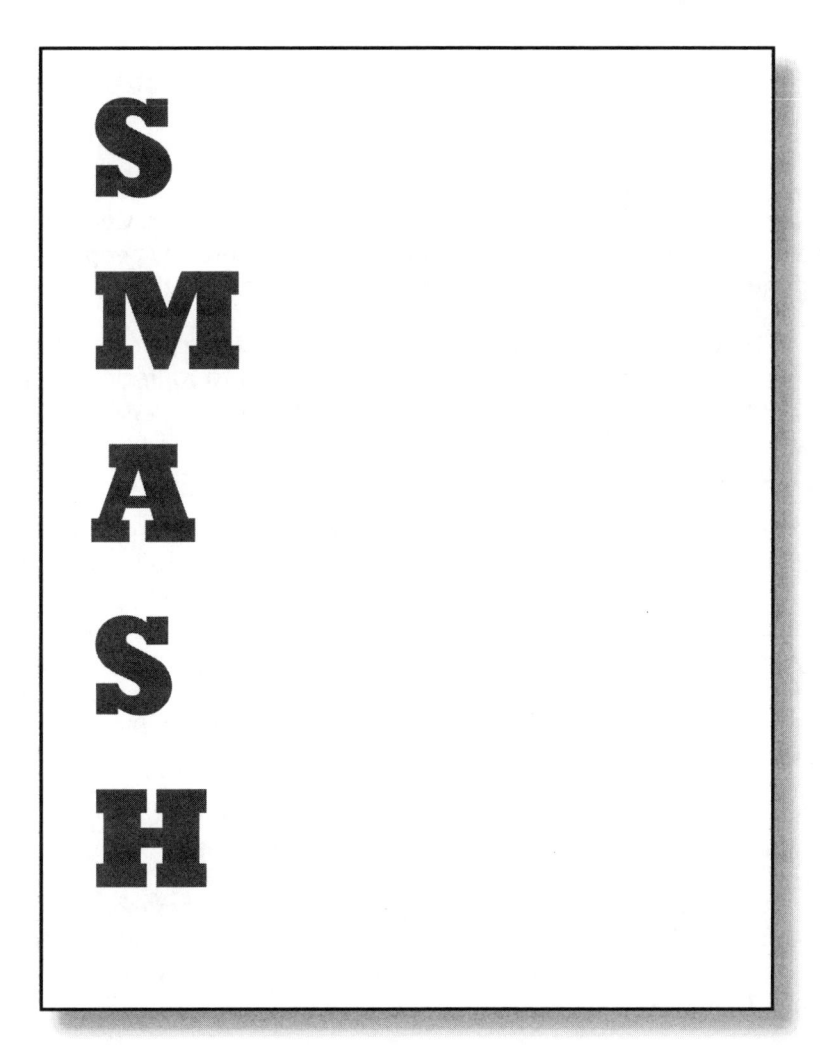

S
M
A
S
H

☐ ☐ ☐ SPIES AND ALLIES

Author: Scott Enebo

Description: This is an activity that gets participants moving and thinking about group dynamics. I like to use this activity to get people to think about their role within their organization and see how they add or detract from the work environment. This can also be used to explore difficult topics within an organization like sexual harassment or cultural inclusion.

Objective: To encourage participants to think about the importance of taking an active role in the events that happen every day in the office and in life.

Audience: Any training audience

Group Size: 15-100

Materials: None

Process:

1. Say, "There are two important rules of this game. First, it is a SILENT activity. No talking from this point forward! Second, this is a 'no contact' game. When I say go, I am going to ask you to start walking quietly around the room without bumping into any people or tables. Just keep moving around each other without touching anyone. Go."

2. Say, "Now, as you are walking, I want you to choose one person in this room in your mind. DO NOT let them know you chose them, just keep it to yourself – this person is your Person A. Everyone has chosen someone in their mind? Nod yes as you walk. Okay, good. Now, keep walking quietly, and choose another person in your mind. Don't let the person know, just keep it to yourself. This person is your Person B."

3. Say, "Now everyone has two people chosen, your Person A and your Person B. Don't let them know you chose them. Now everyone freeze where you are for a moment and look at me. This activity is called 'Spies and Allies'—your Person A is your Ally and your Person B is your Spy. When I say go, I want you to as quickly and QUIETLY as you can, walk so your Ally (person A) is between you and your Spy (person B) in this room. Your ally should be between you and your spy at all times, without bumping into anyone else in the room. Remember, Person A is the Ally, Person B is the Spy. The game will stop when I raise my hand, and if you see my hand raised, stop moving and raise your hand. Ready? GO."

   NOTE: This activity can get people stuck into a corner pretty quickly. After a minute or so, or if the group gets stuck right away, have them stop, and just start mingling around the room again.

4. Say, "Okay. We are going to try this again. Keep walking around as I talk like we did at the beginning. This time when I say go, I want you to REVERSE your Spy and Your Ally, so now Person B is the Ally and Person A is the Spy. You will keep your NEW ally between you and your spy at all times. Ready, GO."

Debrief: To debrief, say this to the whole class:

1. When I say go, I want everyone to point to their Person A, the first ally they chose. Ready, go.

2. Now everybody point to your B, your second ally. Ready, go.

3. If you could tell right away during the game that you were somebody's ally or spy, raise your hand. Those of you with hands raised, how did you know? How could you tell you were an ally or a spy?

4. You knew your spy and your ally, so what was your role in this activity?

5. What did the other people represent for you?

6. Where have you seen this happen in your work?

7. How does this activity inform the work that you do every day?

8. What is one action that you can take to implement what we talked about today, and what difference do you envision that making?

Variations: This activity can be a great way to talk about harassment in the workplace and what it means to be a victim, an instigator or a bystander in an encounter. Simply change the questions to help extrapolate the issues that you are encountering in your workplace.

http://bit.ly/SCORE3SA

SCORE III: SUPER CLOSERS, OPENERS, REVISITERS AND ENERGIZERS

Openers

Most training events and presentations don't have an opener, they just start. The trainer or presenter says something like "Well, we've got lots to cover today, so let's go!" or "Our time is short, so let's get started."

Great trainers and presenters recognize that the opening of their event is some of their most precious real estate, so they take the time to cultivate a learning atmosphere. They "prepare the soil of the mind" before planting the seeds of learning. To do this, they recognize that they must "raise the BAR" with a good opener. They know to **B**reak preoccupation, **A**llow networking, and **R**elate to the content.

Break preoccupation. Participants come to meetings, presentations and learning events with all kinds of distractions, such as how much work they have to do today, what emails and voicemails are piling up while they attend this event, what personal or family issues they should be resolving, or what happened that morning on the job. For this reason, a good presenter recognizes that he or she must break through this preoccupation barrier because it can be the biggest enemy to capturing the full attention of the participants. The key to breaking preoccupation is involvement. Participants can ignore the presenter, but it is difficult to ignore peers when there is a task to accomplish.

Allow networking. Adults usually come to learning events with some experience in the topic. The good presenter will want to tap into that experience throughout the presentation. To accommodate this, he or she will get the participants acquainted with and comfortable with each other. Then throughout the session, the presenter will have them share ideas and experiences with each other thus enhancing the learning for all. Most adults don't want to attend a "sit and get" event; they want to take part, think, contribute and learn.

Networking also reduces tension. Participants come into a learning environment wondering "Can I contribute? Will I fit in? Will anything make me look or feel foolish?" The faster they get comfortable with each other, the faster they will be open to learning.

Relate to the topic. Most of your participants want practical take-away value. To demonstrate this value right from the start, the strong presenter will begin with an opener that relates to the content. Poor presenters often start with a story or a joke that might be funny but has nothing to do with the content of the event. Make sure that your opener has a connection to the topic at hand.

Break preoccupation, allow networking, and relate to the content. By following these three suggestions, you will find that your opening will raise the **BAR** of your presentation, meeting or training event. Following are some time-tested openers that meet these criteria.

http://bit.ly/SCORE3Openers

APPOINTMENT CALENDAR CLOCK

Author: Janice Horne

Description: Use as a get-acquainted opener and also as a setup for revisiting content at various points in your program. This activity is best for multi-day programs.

Objective: To pair up learners with a variety of other participants throughout the program

Audience: Any audience where you want interaction with a variety of participants

Time: 5-10 minutes

Group Size: Up to 50 people

Materials: Clock faces printed on paper or cardstock with blanks for the number of paired interactions you have built into the program.

Process:
1. On the morning of the first day, hand out the clocks.

2. Instruct participants to find another person in the class (not at their table), and fill in one slot on their appointment calendar. For example, if Bob and Becky meet up and decide they will fill in the 1:00 appointment space, Bob would write Becky's name on his clock in the 1:00 space. Becky would write Bob's name in the 1:00 space.

3. Participants then continue moving around the room until they have made appointments with other participants and filled in each of the spaces on the clock. They then return to their seats.

4. Later in the program, whenever you want to pair people up for a revisit or an activity, you would say, "It's time to find your 1:00 appointment (or 3:00, 5:00, etc – wherever you had placed the blanks on the clock)." Participants would then find the person in the group whose name they have in the slot.

5. Have both partners share a key idea they have gained in the training and how they would implement that on the job.

Debrief: Have several participants share a key idea they have gained with the whole group.

Variations: If there is an odd number in the group, assign one person in the group to sign up with 2 others in a time slot.

Super Closers, Openers, Revisiters, Energizers, Volume 3 39

☐ ☐ ☐ **CHOCOLATE PERSONALITIES**

Author: Jaime Pylant

Description: Use this exercise as an opener with a new training class when you would like to assign new groups. It works well when there will be a lot of brainstorming in your session.

Objective: Create new groups with a diverse range of personality types.

Audience: Any training audience

Time: 10-15 minutes

Group Size: 10-50 people

Materials: One bag of Hershey miniatures which contains only Hershey's Chocolate Bar, Hershey's Special Dark Chocolate Bar, Krackel® and Mr. Goodbar®; a timer; and space for four groups to meet.

Process:
1. Ask participants to select their favorite chocolate from the bag.

2. Have participants split into four groups based on the chocolate bar they selected. Feel free to move to a new space in the room.

3. Ask the new groups to discuss for 90 seconds what they like to do outside of work. Are there any commonalities they share?

4. Assign a group leader to each group. The group leader will be the person who last ate chocolate chip pancakes.

5. After 90 seconds, start a large group discussion on the commonalities with each group reporting their findings. Add in the following observations after each group has shared.

    a. Hershey's Chocolate Bars – People who select this tend to be easy going, friendly, patient, dedicated and cooperative

    b. Krackel – People who select this tend to like to try new things and be the class clown while being optimistic, high energy and competitive.

    c. Mr. Goodbar – People who select this tend to like adventure and detail while being dependable, risk-taking and organized.

    d. Dark Chocolate – People who select this tend to be independent, thoughtful, insightful, creative and sensitive.

6. Continue this until each group has finished.

SCORE! III

Debrief: Ask your audience, "Why is this information important to know in training and our environment today?" Listen to some of the answers and drive home the point that we all have different personalities, talents, and experiences, but we're all in this together.

Since we are all different, it wouldn't be beneficial to have all the Hershey Milk Chocolate lovers at one table. Have participants number off to assign new groups.

Variations: Use this as an energizer in the afternoon. The chocolate will help give a shot of energy to the group.

CLINCH THE CLICHÉ ☐ ☐ ☐

Author: Priscilla Shumway

Description: Introduce fun, brainstorming, and team building

Objective: Brainstorm humorous endings to common clichés that help to describe a job, company or process.

Audience: Any training audience

Time: 20 minutes

Group Size: Under 50 people

Materials: One handout with the clichés per person or team.

Process: Have each team complete the cliché to fit your business, training, job, process or company. Tell them to be creative and have fun.

- When you are up to your armpits in alligators it is hard to remember that your initial objective was to_____(drain the swamp).

- The squeaky wheel gets the_____(grease).

- The optimist says the glass is half full. The pessimist says the glass is half empty. The project manager says the glass is _____(twice as big as it needs to be).

- Time is of the _____(essence).

- Don't throw out the baby with the _____(bathwater).

- When you discover that you are riding a dead horse, the best strategy is to _____ (dismount).

- A picture is worth _____(1,000 words).

- A clear conscience is usually the sign of a _____(bad memory).

- 80 percent of output is produced by _____(20 percent of input).

Debrief: Ask each team to share one or two of their clichés.

Variations: Depending on the size of the audience and the amount of time you have, you may have just four or five teams share. Collect their clichés and post throughout the training on PowerPoint™ slides.

Super Closers, Openers, Revisiters, Energizers, Volume 3

☐ ☐ ☐ ICON-KU

Author: Karen Carlson

Description: This is a fun activity for early arrivals to work on that takes zero classroom time.

Objective: Introduce or reinforce commonly used icons related to the course content or to the company or job role.

Audience: Any training audience

Time: 5-10 minutes prior to class

Group Size: Any size

Materials: One game sheet per person

Process: This game is played like the Japanese number placement game Sudoku but with pictures instead of numbers.

1. Use the template to insert icons that represent your company's products or brands or concepts from class. The fewer icons you provide on the game sheet, the harder it will be to complete. (The template game should be easy to complete.) Try to choose icons that can easily be drawn by the participants.

2. Instruct each participant to place an icon in each empty box so that each row, column and nine-box grid contains only one of each icon.

Variations:
1. Use icons that fit the theme of the course like the sample provided which reflects a sports theme.

2. Use commonly used acronyms instead of icons.

---

44   SCORE! III

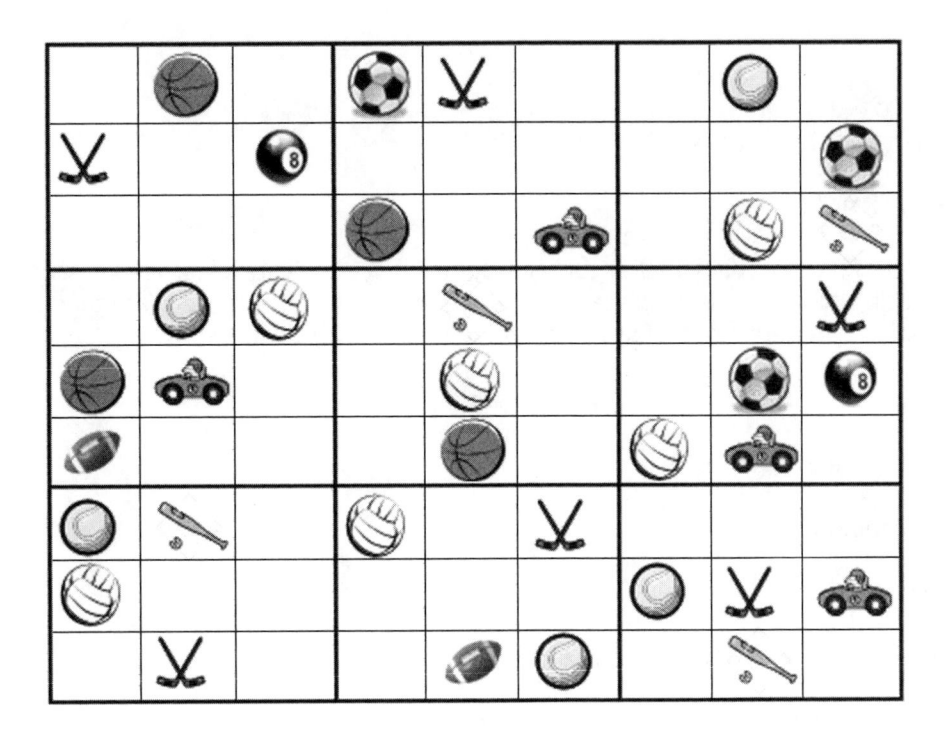

Icon Key:

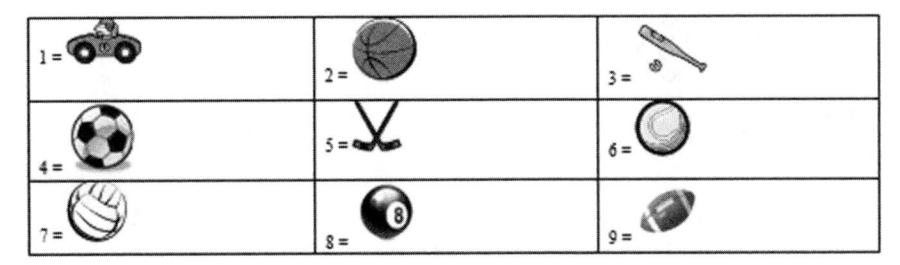

1 = 🏎 (car)	2 = 🏀 (basketball)	3 = 🏏 (bat)
4 = ⚽ (soccer)	5 = 🏒 (hockey sticks)	6 = ⚾ (baseball)
7 = 🏐 (volleyball)	8 = 🎱 (8-ball)	9 = 🏈 (football)

Icon-Ku Answer Key

Replace #s with symbols or acronyms to fit your company or program.

3	2	1	4	5	7	8	6	9
5	7	8	9	6	3	1	2	4
4	9	6	2	8	1	5	7	3
8	6	7	1	3	4	2	9	5
2	1	5	6	7	9	3	4	8
9	4	3	5	2	8	7	1	6
6	3	4	7	1	5	9	8	2
7	8	9	3	4	2	6	5	1
1	5	2	8	9	6	4	3	7

Super Closers, Openers, Revisiters, Energizers, Volume 3 45

LEARNING MASCOT

Author: Marc Ratcliffe

Description: This is a tactile activity that encourages participants to create a learning mascot to support their learning. It also serves to break preoccupation as it is an opening activity that is unusual enough to spark their interest but relevant enough to maintain engagement.

Objective: Create a learning mascot to support learning.

Audience: Any training audience

Time: 5-10 minutes

Group Size: Any size

Materials: At least two colored pipe cleaners per participant

Process:

1. Explain to the participants that they are going to create a "learning mascot" to kick start the session.

2. Provide the participants with a range of colored pipe cleaners and then model the following steps to create a basic human figure:

   Step 1: Create a "V" shape with the pipe cleaner. Make a small loop at the top for the head.

   Step 2: Twist the pipe cleaner five times to make the "body" figure. The remaining two sides will become the legs.

   Step 3: Select a different colored pipe cleaner and bend in half. This will become the arms.

   Step 4: Place the second pipe cleaner in the middle of the "body" of the first pipe cleaner and wrap around each side three to five times.

   You now have a basic person as your learning mascot!

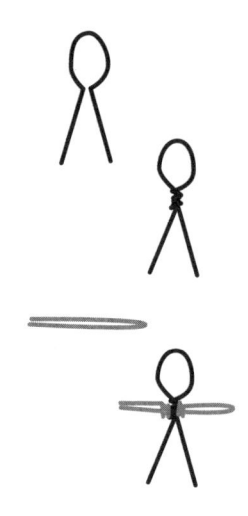

3. Once the demonstration is complete, the trainer should encourage the participants to get creative and make their own using the resources provided.

4. While the participants are creating their own learning mascots, the trainer should prepare the following basic figure on the board or flipchart and label with "head," "heart" and "hands."

```
        Head

Hands        Heart
```

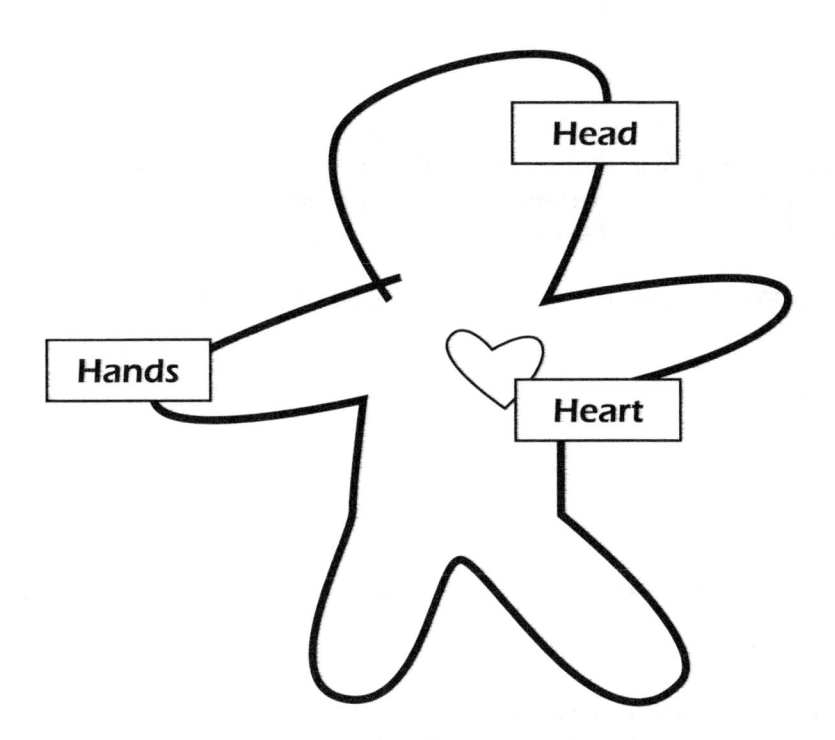

Debrief: Once the participants have completed their learning mascots, the trainer should explain that not only are they mascots, but they are reminders for what the participants will take from the day: The Cognitive (Head), the Affective (Heart) and the Psychomotor (Hands).

As a closer, the trainer can prompt participants at the end of the day to consider what they have learned that relates to what they know, what they can do and what they can feel.

Variations:
1. The mascots can be used as holders for name tags or name tents which gives them life after the first day.

2. Allow the participants to come up with any type of learning mascot (other than a person). It could be a bird, a spider, fish, dog, etc. Then ask them to create a metaphor for learning using their mascot. For example, a fish could signify that knowledge is like an ocean and we have much to explore if we just keep swimming.

3. The learning mascot could be created as part of a team challenge at tables and could be a fun way for participants to commence the grouping process.

Super Closers, Openers, Revisiters, Energizers, Volume 3

MIRROR IMAGE

Author: Scott Enebo

Description: Use this activity to encourage learners to try new things and to trust themselves in new situations. If you are introducing a process or a system that you believe people may be reluctant to attempt, this can give them the confidence to give it a try.

Objective: To demonstrate the power that we have as individuals to do things that we may not be sure we can do.

Audience: Any training audience

Time: 10 minutes

Group Size: Any size

Materials: Flip chart paper, markers (ideal); blank paper and writing instrument (second option)

Process:
1. Ask participants to stand in front of the chart paper and place a marker in each hand.

2. Say, "I am going to give you some instructions and, without thinking or hesitating, I would like you to try to accomplish the task. Again, don't hesitate, just do it. What I would like to ask you to do is, with your dominant hand, write your name in cursive while at the same time writing your name with your non-dominant hand in a mirror image next to that of your dominant hand. Go!"

Note: The product that you are trying to explain will look like the image below.

3. Allow everyone the opportunity to try.

Debrief:
1. What words did you hear from others while they tried this task?
2. What was your initial reaction when you heard what you were to do?
3. What was your reaction after making the attempt?
4. What did you think about if you were not the first person to try this?
5. How have you experienced something like this before?
6. How does this concept relate to what we are doing at work right now?
7. What can we do to encourage change that seems daunting at first?

Variations:
1. This activity may also be done blindfolded. While many of the debrief questions can stay the same, this adds another layer of envisioning success and trusting our instincts as we try and accomplish tasks.
2. As a revisit, instead of asking the debrief questions, ask participants to share something that they are going to "mirror" back when they are on the job.

http://bit.ly/SCORE3MI

PAPER BALANCING

Author: Priscilla Shumway

Description: Juggle or balance a single sheet of 8½"x11" piece of paper on one finger for a minimum of 3 seconds.

Objective: This exercise gets participants thinking outside of the box and problem solving.

Audience: Any training audience

Time: 4 minutes

Group Size: Any size

Materials: One 8½"x11" sheet of paper per person

Process:
1. Hand out an 8½"x11" sheet of paper to each person.
2. Have everyone stand.
3. Say, "Figure out a way to balance this paper on one of the four existing corners on one finger for a minimum of 3 seconds. You must balance the entire paper."
4. Play music.
5. As people solve it, clap and have others look at the solutions.
6. After 2 minutes, show them the easiest solution. Make one fold from one of the corners. Open up the fold and balance it on a finger. By opening the fold, you have created an air foil or sail effect and can balance the paper for a longer period of time.

Debrief: Most people will get very complicated with their solutions. The simplest solution is often the best. Ask them to brainstorm as a team how they might make this activity relevant to their training content. Look for:

- Thinking outside of the box
- Looking for more than one solution to a problem
- Finding balance in work and family life
- If you have very technical or difficult information, participants may think it is impossible for them to succeed.
- With some simple tips and guidance from the instructor, the impossible will become possible. Why did no one ask for help? The instructor knows how to do it. Ask him or her.

Variations: You can impose more rules to the activity such as you cannot hold it in your mouth, you cannot ask a friend to hold it for you, or you cannot tape it to a table. This gets laughs, but it also stifles some of the more creative solutions.

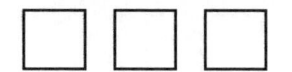

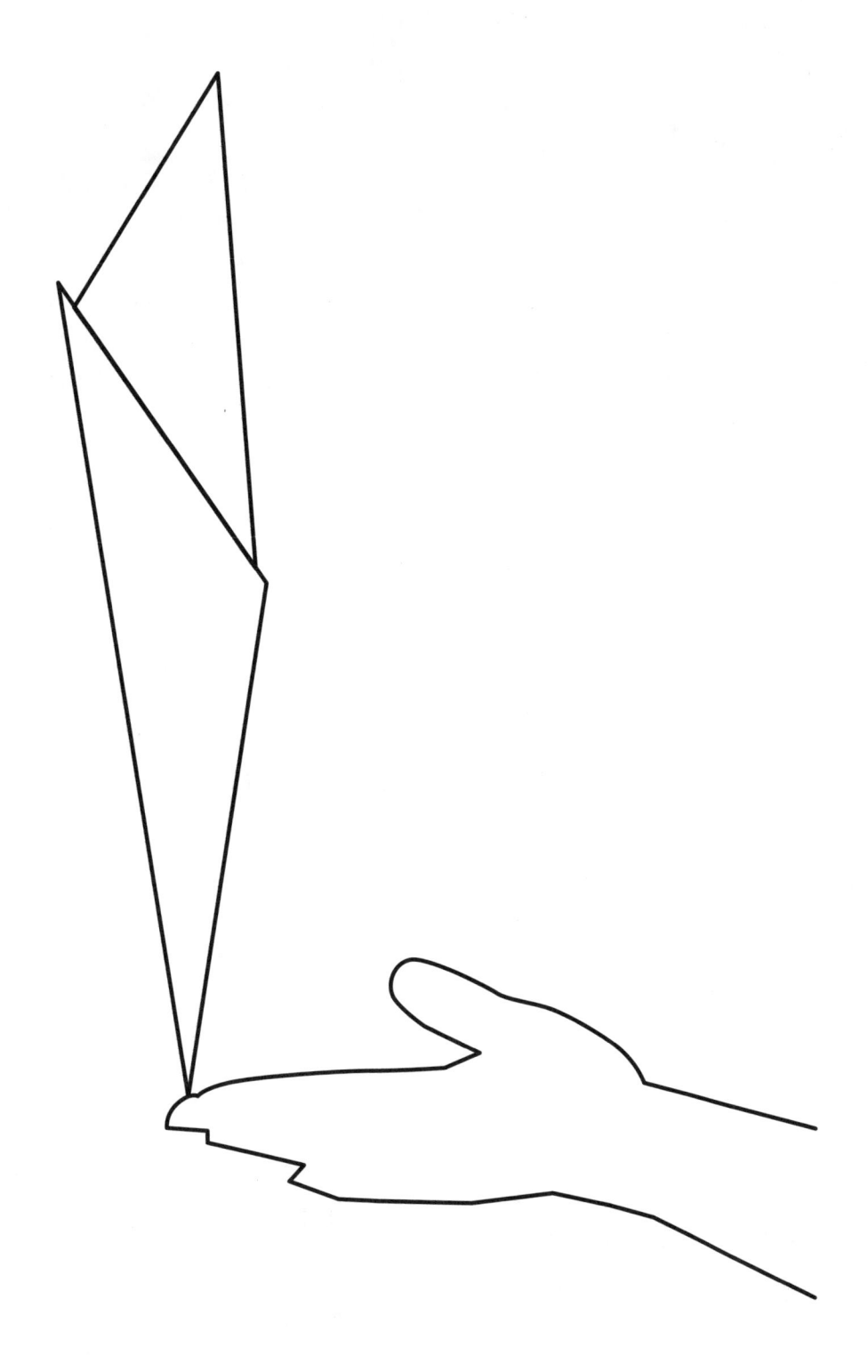

Super Closers, Openers, Revisiters, Energizers, Volume 3   51

ROBBED MUSEUM

Author: Jaime Pylant

Description: Once, when I was teaching a two-day Train-the-Trainer Boot Camp for The Bob Pike Group, the overnight hotel staff threw away every single poster created on Day 1. So, at the beginning of Day 2, I had my class quickly recreate as many posters as they could remember from the previous day, and thus "Robbed Museum" was born. This activity allows you to revisit covered material without saying "Let's review." My class got 90 percent of the posters back on the wall. The few they missed, I was able to quickly recreate and discuss with them.

Objective: Revisit content illustrated on a poster by having participants recreate the original.

Audience: Any training or learning audience that has been in class for at least one day

Time: 10-15 minutes

Group Size: Any size

Materials: Markers, posters, tape, timer

Process: Set this activity up for success by creating posters and reviewing their content the day before.

1. Tell your class that the classroom was robbed overnight, and they took all of our beautiful pieces of art off our wall.

2. As a class, your task is to replace every single poster that was on the wall.

3. You will have markers, posters, tape, and 5 minutes to recreate our art gallery.

Debrief: Have participants stand by their favorite poster creation and explain why they liked the poster and what information is being displayed.

Variations: Have the class break into small groups of 3-6 people. Assign a group leader to be curator for each group and have them recreate everything as a small group. You can then debrief the same way; however, you will have multiple recreations of the same posters.

http://bit.ly/SCORE3SN

STANDARDS AND NORMS ☐ ☐ ☐

Author: Bob Pike

Description: Use this activity to allow the group to establish their own ground rules for the training.

Objective: To create ownership by the participants around ground rules for the training

Audience: Any training audience

Time: 10-15 minutes

Group Size: Best for groups of 10 or more (in subgroups of 5 people)

Materials: One pad of sticky notes for each group, a felt tip marker, two sheets of chart paper posted on the walls

Process:
1. Each table is asked to divide participants into two approximately equal groups. One group will be the "I" group, the other will be the "P" group.

2. Each group is given a pad of sticky notes and a marker.

3. The groups are then told that "I" stands for Instructor. "P" stands for participant. Then say, "You have 3 minutes to come up with five guidelines for you as participants to follow to help each other get the most from this program or that I, as the instructor, can follow to make sure that you get the most from the program." Share an example for each category such as "If you are a P group, one of your guidelines might be that there should be no side bar conversations. If you are an I group, one of your guidelines might be that the instructor should allow at least 10 minutes for Q&A [questions and answers] every 90 minutes."

4. After 3 minutes, all of the I groups in the room meet at a poster on one wall and print "Instructor Guidelines" at the top and then merge their guidelines into a total of 10 guidelines to follow.

5. P groups do the same thing on the opposite wall. After 3 minutes, have the I's present their guidelines to the rest of the groups. Groups can suggest additional guidelines.

6. Follow the same process with the P's. Then, as an instructor say, "I am willing to commit to following all these guidelines, if each of you as participants agrees to follow the participant guidelines. Do we have an agreement?"

    Note: There are times when you may want to add a guideline to the P chart. For example, if the group has not said anything about cell phone usage or texting during class, ask that this guideline be added.

7. After two hours and periodically throughout the rest of the class, stop and ask each table to discuss and come up with a score from 1-7 for both the instructor and the participants (1 is low and 7 is high). Post the average of these scores on the respective charts. If we do not have 7s, ask the groups what you, as the instructor, need to do or change to improve to get a 7, as well as what each participant needs to do or change so that they feel they can give themselves a 7 as a group.

Super Closers, Openers, Revisiters, Energizers, Volume 3

☐ ☐ ☐ # SUPERHERO SORTING

Author: Adrianne Roggenbuck

Description: This opener will gauge the different knowledge and experience levels of the audience. It is a good opener for a session that has a flexible flow and is easy to modify to meet the needs of the group.

Objective: Participants will self-evaluate their level of mastery of the content prior to the start of the content delivery. They will also outline key concepts and suggest a variety of processes.

Audience: Any group where there is a wide range of experience or knowledge levels of the content.

Time: 20 minutes

Group Size: This is best suited for groups of 20-30 people, divided into small groups of 3-7 participants each.

Materials: Chart paper, tape, markers

Process:
1. Have the entire group think about their current knowledge of today's content. Would they consider themselves novices, experts or somewhere in between? They are going to split into three groups. If they are well versed enough to share the content with others, then they are in the Superman group. If they have little or no knowledge of the content, they will be in the Spider-Man group. If they have some knowledge but are not totally comfortable with the content, then they are in the Elasti-Girl group.

2. Have them get together with the other superheroes in their group. If the three groups are larger than seven people each, subdivide them.

3. One person from each subgroup will bring markers, one person will get chart paper, and another will get tape to fasten the chart paper to the wall near the group.

4. The Spider-Man group will think about what they need from this session in terms of knowledge and support, because they feel the need to construct a "supporting web" to feel comfortable with the new learning.

5. The Superman group feels confident that they can "fly" with the content so they will think of the key concepts that they would want to impart to the Spider-Man group.

6. The Elasti-Girl group will focus on a slightly different dimension for the day. They will look for things that can be done to make the session "snappy." This could relate to both content and process for the day.

7. Have the groups brainstorm for 4½ minutes and then start creating a poster to share their thoughts with the whole group. They will have an additional 3 minutes to create their poster.

8. The groups will select a spokesperson to present the information they recorded to the whole group.

9. Determine which items will be addressed in the session and what can be added to either the content or process. Some flexibility is required here on the part of the facilitator. Not every suggestion will be able to be woven in, so do not over-promise and under-deliver.

Debrief: Say, " This activity honors the expertise in the room and helps each group recognize the needs of the other groups. Today we will band together as superheroes to make this session valuable for each of us."

Variations:
1. The groups could be numbered 1, 2, 3 instead of named, or the names could be changed to fit a different theme.

2. These groups could be the basis for regrouping the participants later. They could form new groups that have at least one Superman, one Elasti-Girl, and one Spider-Man. This would mix the ability levels for an activity or discussion.

http://bit.ly/SCORE3SS

☐ ☐ ☐ T PUZZLE

Author: Janice Horne

Description: Put the puzzle together as a table group and use it to make a link to your message or topic. This activity can be used to introduce a process or skill or can be used to reinforce teamwork.

Objective: Raise awareness for your message or topic, especially when the topic may seem to be complex or is new.

Audience: Technical, process-driven

Time: 5-10 minutes

Group Size: Under 50 with small table groupings of 5-7 people

Materials: T Puzzle (shown) copied onto cardstock and cut out.

Process: Place one puzzle on each table. Invite participants at a table to cooperate to put the puzzle pieces together to make a capital letter "T." Pieces may not be overlapped. All pieces will be used. When one table solves the puzzle, those members should stand up and help those at other tables.

Debrief:
1. Have participants hold a small group discussion at their table. They should discuss their observations from the activity such as what made it hard or easy and how they approached solving the puzzle as a team.

2. Debrief by hearing one observation from each table. One response you are looking for is that they felt they didn't have all the pieces. If, after all groups have shared, no one says they didn't feel like they had all the pieces, then ask the question "Did anyone think that you weren't given all the pieces to the puzzle?"

3. Then say, "Today as we begin to get into this new (process, skill, learning), I guarantee that you will be given all the pieces you need to complete (this process, skill, learning) successfully. And even though, like this puzzle, the new (process, skill, learning) may look daunting at first, the more times you practice, the easier it will become, just like the more times you put this puzzle together the easier it will become."

4. Make any other links between the puzzle and your topic or message that you believe are relevant.

Variations: 1. To make the activity move faster, place words that go across multiple pieces or create other clues on the pieces that make the puzzle easier to complete. Do this on only one puzzle and place it at a single table. Then have the table that finishes first help other tables.

2. Use this activity as a closer to emphasize that they have all the pieces to complete the new process. Now it will just require practice to make it easier.

3. Use the activity as an opener, and then repeat it as a closer to come full circle.

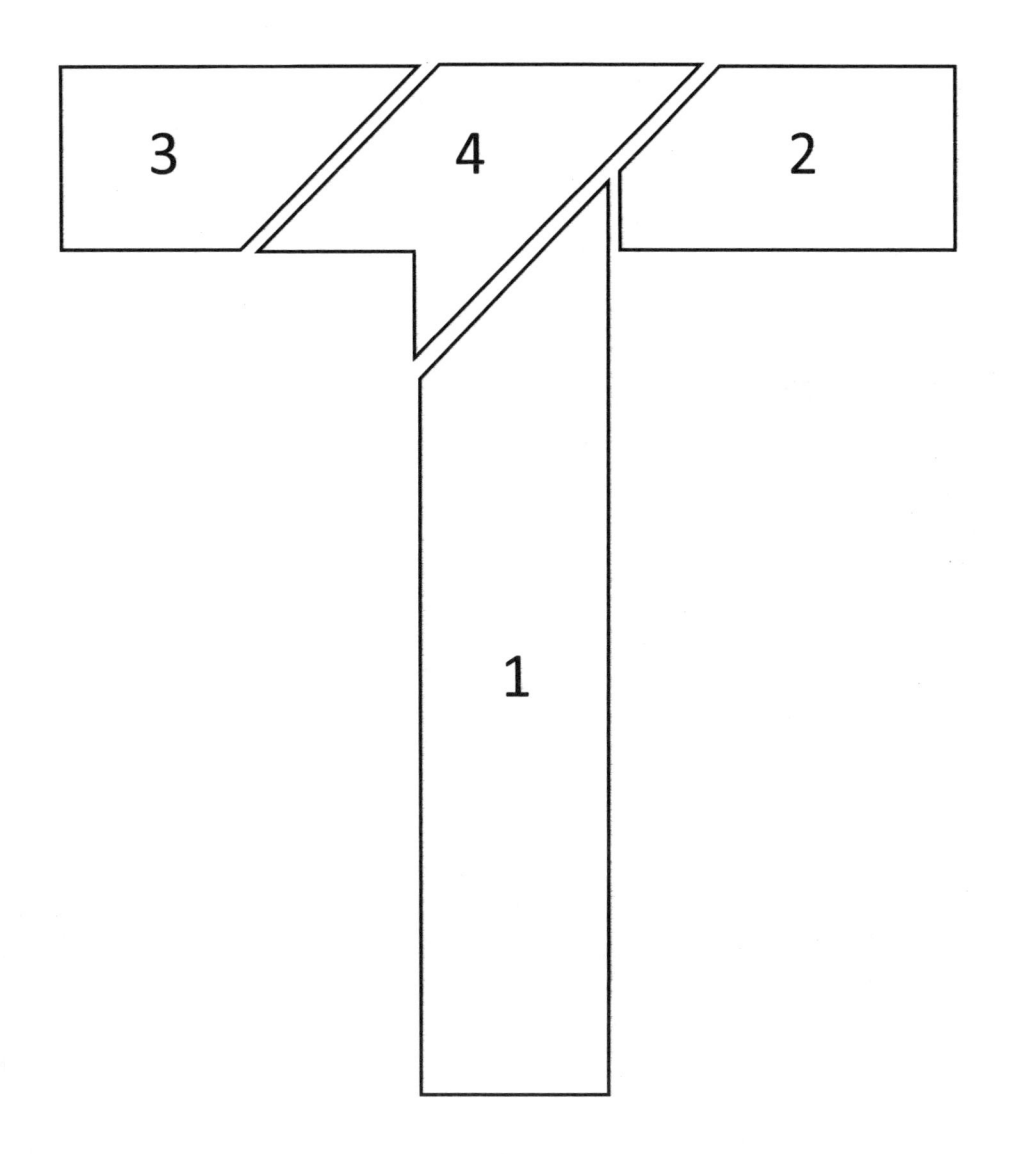

WE'RE A PUZZLE, BUT STILL A TEAM ☐ ☐ ☐

Author: Jaime Pylant

Description: This is an absolutely wonderful way to illustrate teamwork and energize your audience whether the learners are strangers or have worked together for many years. If you have multiple teams from the same organization, this helps illustrate they are both working toward the same goal.

Objective: The learner will experience teamwork through a kinesthetic activity.

Audience: Any training audience that can be easily divided into four groups

Time: 10-15 minutes

Group Size: 4-50 people

Materials: One 100-piece puzzle, PowerPoint slide with a picture of the puzzle, sealable plastic bags, timer, table space.

Process:
1. Put together the puzzle ahead of time.
2. Divide the intact puzzle into four quadrants and separate.
3. Using separate sealable bags, dismantle the puzzle and place an individual quadrant into each bag.
4. Seal the bags.
5. Tell the class their assignment is to complete this puzzle in 5 minutes.
6. Display the picture of your puzzle.
7. Each group will compete against each other to see who can complete the puzzle the fastest.
8. Distribute sealed bags, but have participants wait to open.
9. Once every group has its bag and is ready, have them begin.

Debrief: By the end of the activity, participants will realize their puzzle pieces create only one-fourth of the puzzle. Each group must complete their portion and then add it to the other groups' portions to complete the final product.

Then ask participants, "How does this activity relate to our work environment at Company XYZ?"

Variations: Once all the bags have been filled with one-quarter of the puzzle, take one or two pieces from each bag, and place them into another group's bag. Do this for all four. Now, when the groups are racing to complete their puzzle, they'll find pieces that do not fit anywhere with their picture. As each group discovers this, they'll learn they must swap out pieces illustrating the point that everyone's role on the team is to accomplish the group's mission regardless of their assigned role and team.

WHICH IS MORE IMPORTANT? ☐ ☐ ☐

Author: Ayako Nakamura

Description: This exercise illustrates that there is equality between two items or topics.

Objective: To illustrate that two things we are going to learn about today are equally important

Audience: Any training audience

Time: 1-2 minutes

Group Size: Any size

Materials: None

Process:
1. Ask participants, "When you do a presentation, which do you think is more important: the content or the process?" (Or insert your two content pieces into the question.) Pause a few seconds. Say, "Let's look at it this way. Let's assume your right hand represents the content, and your left hand represents the process."

2. Hold your hands in front of you, and be ready to clap. Ask all participants to do the same. Say, "Again, the content is your right hand and the process is your left hand, and we are asking ourselves which is more important. In just a moment, I will say, '1, 2, 3', and then at the 3, you will all clap. Ready? 1, 2, 3!"

3. Ask, "Which of your hands created the sound? You are probably thinking 'Both hands, of course!' And you are right. You need both hands to create a sound! That means we need to have both good content and good process for effective presentations, and that is what we will focus on today."

Debrief: Ask the group why it is important to have both good content and a good process. Get several responses and reinforce the idea that both are important.

Variations: The content and the process can be changed to anything – two things that both need to be good related to your training topic. Examples include task accomplishment and people growth for coaching or mentoring training, or product knowledge and sales skills for sales training.

WHICH WORDS?

Author: Adrianne Roggenbuck

Description: This can be used either as an opener to introduce new content or as an energizer to use when the group needs to be engaged. Depending on the question you choose for the group to answer, it could also be used as a closer.

Objective: To introduce new content by having the participants make their own connection to the topic, or to energize the group in an engaging way. When used as a closer, participants are drawing conclusions or summarizing key content.

Audience: Any training audience

Time: 10 minutes

Group Size: Any size, but will work best if the group is divided into smaller groups of 4-6 people. This would also make a good partner activity.

Materials: A PowerPoint slide or poster with the Top Ten list on it, a timer

Process:
1. Divide the large group into smaller teams of 4-6 people or into pairs if there are fewer than 10 people.
2. Challenge the teams to create a list of the top 10 most common nouns in the English language.
3. Put on a timer for 2½ minutes.
4. When time is up, share the Top 10 list. Each team receives one point for each of their nouns that appears on the master list. Award two points if the word is in the same numbered slot as the master list.
5. Have teams total their points and record them.
6. The next part of the challenge is to use as many words from the list as they can to answer this question, "What does today's topic mean to you?" They will work together with their partner or small group to craft their answer.

Debrief:
1. Share the answers with the whole group. Award points for the number of words used in the description and add these points to the previous total to determine the winning team. You may choose to add bonus points for teams whose answers make sense and really answer the question coherently. Prizes may be awarded to the winning team.
2. Tell the group that by doing this activity, they were forced to think beyond just themselves to find connections between today's topic and the world. This will help them to see that their learning has an impact not only on themselves, but also creates a ripple effect that could have far-reaching consequences.

Variations: A different question for step six in the process may be used depending on the purpose of the activity. For example:

1. What are the benefits of today's topic?
2. How would you implement today's topic?
3. What are the key takeaways from today's session?
4. How will today's topic improve your skill level/ job/life?
5. How does today's topic relate to any of these words?
6. Write three learning goals for yourself that incorporate at least five of these words.

The Top Ten nouns in English:

1. Time
2. Person
3. Year
4. Way
5. Day
6. Thing
7. Man
8. World
9. Life
10. Hand

Taken from the *Top Ten of Everything 2012* by Caroline Ash and Alexander Ash, Sterling Publishing, Sterling, NY.

http://bit.ly/SCORE3WW

SCORE III: SUPER CLOSERS, OPENERS, REVISITERS AND ENERGIZERS

REVISITERS

Albert Mehrabian, professor emeritus of psychology at UCLA, did a study to determine how often a person needs to be exposed to ideas in order to remember the majority of them. His research determined the following:

If you are exposed to an idea one time, retention is less than 10 percent after 30 days.

If you are exposed to an idea six times, retention is greater than 90 percent after 30 days (especially if there is interval reinforcement which means revisiting the idea after an hour, after a day, after three days, after a week, etc.)

Mehrabian's research suggests that, to help people learn, we need to cover a concept or idea at least six times while allowing some time lapse in between the reviews. Yet most learning events today cover ideas one time and expect the participants to remember them. Maybe the reason this happens is that trainers believe that it is boring to repeat themselves over and over.

But doing a revisit doesn't have to be boring. Creative trainers and presenters find interesting ways to allow the participants to do the revisiting thus making it more interesting and effective. So here's the key: review is when the trainer does it, and a revisit is when the participants do it. Therein lies the power – getting the participants to revisit.

Here are some tips for helping participants learn more in your sessions:

- Revisit early and often. Remember, we need to cover key content at least six times for maximum retention.

- Don't call it "review." In our sessions, we suggest that trainers avoid the "R" word (review) and instead use the word revisit.

- Use a variety of revisiting techniques. This keeps the interest level of participants high and helps them to stay engaged in the learning process.

The following pages contain some of our favorite revisiting techniques. Enjoy learning and employing these techniques, knowing that ultimately your learners will be the ones to benefit!

http://bit.ly/SCORE3Revisiters

BOARD GAME RE-DO ☐ ☐ ☐

Author: Karen Carlson

Description: Use this activity to revisit and celebrate knowledge gained during the class.

Objective: Encourage healthy competition while reinforcing learning concepts during a multi-day course.

Audience: Any training audience

Time: When using as a revisiter, allow 3 minutes per round, and do several rounds throughout the course

Group Size: 4 people per group

Materials: Board games and playing pieces (one game board per table), double stick tape or poster putty, index cards or sticky notes, small prizes (optional)

Process: Recycle old board games from your closet or purchase at a discount store and adapt the rules to fit your content. Board games that work particularly well include: Sorry!™, Monopoly™, Candy Land™, or Trouble™.

1. Prior to breaks or during lunch, encourage participants to submit questions pertaining to the course content by writing the question on one side of an index card or sticky note and an answer on the other side. (You may want to review questions and answers for accuracy prior to using them.)

2. Periodically through the multi-day course, have teams play the game for 3 minutes. Participants roll the dice or choose a color card (Candy Land) and need to correctly answer a question related to the training to move ahead the appropriate number of spaces.

3. Participants can use double-stick tape or poster putty to affix playing pieces to the board game once each round is done. The person closest to the finish line wins at the end of all of the rounds (this will vary by game board).

Debrief: Discuss any questions that participants had trouble answering.

Variations: If using as a closer, allow teams to play the game for 7 minutes. Award a small prize, if desired, to the winner at each table.

CARD QUESTIONS

Author: Bob Pike

Description: Ask participants to create questions from the content covered, and then use these cards as a revisit for the content.

Objective: To revisit key content and close a content section

Audience: Any training audience

Time: 5-6 minutes

Group Size: Any size divided into subgroups of 5-7 people

Materials: One or two 3"x5" cards per person

Process: As you near a break, especially a lunch break, give each participant one or two index cards. Tell them that they "earn their way to break" by writing down two questions that they think everyone should be able to answer about the content covered during the training "up until now." (Note: you can also select a specific time period like "in the last module," "this morning," etc.) The questions can be true/false, multiple choice, short answer or fill-in-the blank. The question and choices (if any) go on the front of the card, and the answers go on the back.

After 2 minutes, have each person share his or her question(s) with his or her group and have the group answer them. This activity stands alone, but it can also be used with the variations shown below.

Variations:

1. Use the Card Questions developed in part 1 above. After the break, have groups choose a new group leader. Have each group choose their best five questions out of all the questions they generated before the break. Have the group leader take the cards to the next table and "test the table." The questions are asked by the group leader and the new group collaborates to answer the questions. Rotate so that each group gets to answer all the questions.

2. Have all group leaders turn their cards into the instructor. Use this method several times during your training so that you can then develop a quiz from the top 10 or 20 questions.

3. Each participant is given a card and is given one minute to write his or her name on the front, and the single most important thing learned during the class and how he or she plans to use it.

    1. Participants are each given a card and one minute to write their names on the front of the card and the single most important thing they've learned during the class and how they plan to use it.

    2. After a minute, all the cards are passed to one person in the group. This person redistributes the cards so that no one at the table has his or her own card.

    3. On the back of the card, each person has one minute to complete this sentence about the person who owns the card: One contribution that [name] has made to us during this training is _____.

    4. After a minute, the person that distributed the cards starts the round robin process by saying: "I have [name's] card. Here's what he or she plans to do," and then reads aloud the sentence the person wrote on the front of the card. The reader then turns the card over and reads the praise sentence about the person. The reader then hands the card to its owner. The owner is only allowed to say, "Thank you."

    5. Then the owner of that first card repeats the process with the card he or she received. This continues until everyone in the group has their own card back.

http://bit.ly/SCORE3CQ

☐ ☐ ☐ CONFOUNDED

Author: Janice Horne

Description: Participants revisit content to form questions and then answer questions for rewards.

Objective: Revisit information to enhance retention

Audience: Any training audience

Time: Initial card creation – 10 minutes; Revisits 5 – 10 minutes each

Group Size: Under 50 in table groups of 5-7 people

Materials: 3"x5" cards

Process:
1. In advance, write six questions on 3"x5" cards – two easy (E), two moderate (M), and two difficult (D) questions about your topic. Label the questions E, M, or D.

2. Then inform the participants that they will have an opportunity to create some of their own quiz questions.

3. Invite each table to discuss questions they can ask from the course content. (The answers must have been covered in class or found in course materials.)

4. Each table needs to come up with six questions of varying degrees of difficulty and then write each question on one side of a 3"x5" card and the answer on the back. Each question goes on a separate card:

   A. Two easy questions (participants should know the answers without looking in the materials)

   B. Two medium difficulty questions (participants may need to refer to materials to answer the questions)

   C. Two difficult questions (most likely will require referring to materials)

5. Participants note on the front of each card whether the question is E (easy), M (moderate), or D (difficult).

6. Allow 6 minutes for the activity.

7. Collect the cards. Mix in your cards.

8. Sort the cards into three piles: easy, moderate, and difficult.

9. Inform participants that they will have an opportunity to answer questions and earn rewards at intervals throughout the session.

10. Throughout the session, the trainer can announce "pop quiz." Each table group decides if they want an easy, moderate or difficult question. If answered correctly, the group earns point values that the trainer has previously assigned.

11. Easy questions should be answered within 15 seconds; moderate within 30 seconds; difficult questions within 60 seconds.

12. If the question is answered correctly in the given time frame, then the group earns the reward.

13. Conferring with materials is okay and encouraged.

CREATE A MURAL

Author: Karen Carlson

Description: Participants create an artistic representation of the content learned throughout the class; this works best for classes that are at least two days in length.

Objective: Participants work in pairs or groups of no more than four people to create a piece of art that captures key concepts from the class. Pairs will work best for smaller groups.

Audience: Any training audience

Time: 10 minutes

Group Size: 8 or more people divided into smaller groups of no more than four people

Materials: One page of flip chart paper per table or pair, colored markers, tape

Process:
1. Provide each pair or group with one sheet of flip chart paper and several colored markers.
2. Assign each group a portion of the course, such as Day 1, Module 1, etc.
3. Have groups spread throughout the room if possible.
4. Instruct each group to draw images that represent key concepts covered during the time period assigned to them. Key terms or acronyms may be written on the flipchart in addition to art work. Allow 3 minutes for drawing. If more time is needed, add another minute or two.
5. Call time. Ask each group to tape their flip chart page to the wall. Challenge the groups to describe a page created by another group to ensure concepts were captured.

Debrief: Add any key concepts that may have been missed in the drawings. Thank groups for their creativity!

Variations: Divide each flipchart page into sections or columns based on the time periods assigned (one column for Day 1, one column for Day 2, etc.). Have each group create a work of art for only one of the columns. After 3 minutes, call time and have groups pass their art work to the next table and continue drawing in another column on the new flip chart. Repeat until all columns have been completed. Hang the art on the wall and have groups discuss the key concepts represented in their works of art.

DICE OF FATE ☐ ☐ ☐

Author: Ayako Nakamura

Description: On the second day of a multi-day training, ask participants to share what and how they have applied their learning from Day 1, especially if there was some time between Day 1 and 2.

Objective: Share participants' on-the-job applications so they can learn from each other.

Audience: Any training audience

Time: 10 minutes

Group Size: Fewer than 50 people divided into small groups of 5-6 people

Materials: A die for each group

Process:
1. Have a flip chart posted with six numbered topics that you would want participants to know about and be able to share. For example, content from The Bob Pike Group's Train-the-Trainer Boot Camp on Day 1 would include: 1. Opener, 2. Closer, 3. Revisiter, 4. Energizer, 5. 90/20/8, 6. CIO.

2. In each group, one person throws a die, and the number on the die shows the topic that the person shares. For example, if person A throws a 2, then she would share one thing she learned about a closer. When the first person is done, the second person throws the die and does the same.

3. Set the timer for 8 minutes, and each team will continue until time is up.

Variations: The six topics can be anything related to your training content. If Day 1 and Day 2 are back-to-back, then participants can share what they learned from Day 1 or their action plans related to the topic.

MYTH BUSTER

Author: Marc Ratcliffe

Description: Participants will often have pre-conceived ideas, generalizations or social myths about a topic when they enter training. "Myth buster" is a way of confronting these head on while using the data gained from the session to support a new position.

Objective: Check the participants' understanding through their application of knowledge to a series of common myths.

Audience: Beginning or intermediate knowledge level in relation to the content

Time: 20-30 minutes, depending on the number of myths to be busted

Group Size: Any size

Materials: A list of common myths about a topic of your choice.

Process: Identify your myth-busting topic and research some of the common myths. For example, here is a list from Liz Davidson, CEO of Financial Finesse, which she contributed to *Forbes* magazine about investing:

- Myth 1 – You should focus on finding opportunity which could turn into very lucrative "home run" investments.

- Myth 2 – The more you study the market, the better you will do in the market.

- Myth 3 – International investing is too risky; you should stay domestic.

- Myth 4 – Good quarterly or annual returns mean the fund has a good strategy.

- Myth 5 – A more complex investment strategy is better. This is what it takes to beat the market.

Present the list to the participants and ask them to either confirm or debunk the myth using information learned during the session. As an extension, it is a good idea to add some myths which are in fact true to really test their understanding of the topic.

Debrief: Depending on the size of the overall group, facilitate a sharing of the most ideal answers to the myth buster questions. This could include a combination of responses by you and the participants.

Variations:
1. Create different myth sheets for different groups and have them teach back their responses to the other groups. This enables a larger amount of content to be covered and creates a more dynamic interaction between participants.

2. Reverse the process and ask the participants to create the myth busting questions based on topics covered in the session. They would then test their peers as part of the revisit. In this way, it is a "checking for understanding" activity for both the participants creating the questions as well as the ones being asked the questions.

PLAYING CARD QUESTIONS

Author: Janice Horne

Description: This is an informal method of asking quiz or test questions.

Objective: Revisit content to improve retention

Audience: Any training audience

Time: 5-10 minutes

Group Size: Under 50 organized in small table groups of 4-7 people

Materials: Giant playing cards, content questions printed on sticky labels

Process: Affix questions printed on labels to giant playing cards. At different times throughout the class, give participants one or two cards each. If participants can correctly answer the question on the card, they can keep the card. You can then choose a winning hand based on the variations below.

Variations:
1. The person with the best poker hand gets a prize.
2. The person with the most of the same card gets a prize.
3. Table groups which have pooled their cards to form the best hand win a prize.

SAFARI WALL

Author: Marc Ratcliffe

Description: "Safari" is the Swahili word for "journey." This activity creates a structured way of recording key experiences of a learning journey for use at the end of training as a revisiting tool. In many ways, it acts like a timeline for participants to visually identify where they have been and what they have learned along the way.

Objective: Create a visual representation of learning and facilitate reflection of key concepts by participants.

Audience: For any training audience

Time: Ongoing. Allow for 20 minutes for completing as a revisiter at the end of the training.

Group Size: Any size

Materials: Flip chart, sticky notes and colored pens

Process:

1. Set up the activity beforehand by creating your own safari wall using flip charts. Write headings for key topics or experiences from left to right on the wall using colored pens. Leave sufficient space for participants to add their own responses using sticky notes.

2. Introduce the concept of the safari wall to the participants during the opening of the session, including the link to it being the Swahili word for "journey."

3. At different times during the session, direct participants to add items to the safari wall. These could take the form of:

   - Lists of items,
   - Answers to questions or problems,
   - Examples for implementation,
   - Reflections on techniques, or
   - Observations of best practices.

4. At the end of the session, ask the participants to go to the safari wall to have one last look at their shared journey.

Debrief: Ask the participants to consider what the most important information is for their situation and challenge them to remember the context of some of the lists. Encourage participants to add anything additional based on reflection and direct them to write in their own books anything they think is noteworthy as part of a final action planning activity.

Variations:
1. This activity can be easily transformed into an online activity using virtual notice boards and asking participants to review the combined findings at the end of their training.

2. As an extension, the trainer could photograph the safari wall and provide an electronic copy to participants or create a compilation from every group and have a Safari Wall Year Book.

3. The safari wall could be turned into an infographic to support the learning of future groups or added to a social bookmarking site to share with other learners external to the organization.

SHAPE FRIENDS

Author: Ayako Nakamura

Description: Add movements when answering quiz questions

Objective: Energize the participants with quiz questions that require moving about the room

Audience: Any training audience

Time: 5-10 minutes

Group Size: 20-30 people

Materials: Shape cubes (5 different shapes or colors, 20-30 pieces for each shape or color based on the number of participants)

Process:
1. Place all the shape cubes on a table at the back of the classroom. Show a revisiting quiz on the screen from your training content. The quiz should have up to five options for answers. Instead of just labeling A, B, C and so on, label the options as ■♥♦◆ and have each shape be a different color.

2. Participants are asked to go to the back table, pick the shape that represents what they think is the right answer, and get together with other participants who select the same shape. Have them discuss why they think their answer is correct. Show the answer and explain as necessary.

3. Ask the next quiz question and repeat the process.

Variations:
1. You can use this as a networking activity. Ask questions that allow participants to get to know each other, e.g., your training experience ■ less than a year, ♥ 1-3 years, ♦ 4-5 years, ◆ more than 5 years.

2. When participants get together with other participants with the same shape, have them take a few minutes to network, and then ask the next question.

SURVEY SAYS ☐ ☐ ☐

Author: Karen Carlson

Description: Use this activity to get people up and moving while gauging the retention of key concepts of the class.

Objective: Capture key learning points of course content by interviewing other participants

Audience: Any training audience

Time: 5-7 minutes

Group Size: Any size

Materials: Pre-made topic cards or blank index cards, enough for one card per participant

Process:
1. Have each person draw a card from your pre-made topic cards. Instruct them to seek out participants at other tables to capture one learning point per person relating to the topic on the card.

2. Encourage them to move quickly to capture as many concepts as possible.

3. Set the timer for 3 minutes. If time permits, add another minute or two for collecting survey results.

Debrief: Have table groups discuss each person's survey results.

Variations:
1. Have participants choose their own topic based on course content. Each participant writes the topic on a blank index card and uses the card to jot down the survey results from the interviews.

2. Create questions that relate to how the participants will apply the new knowledge or skill to their jobs.

Survey Says...

Topic:

Point 1:

Point 2:

Point 3:

TURN THE CARDS

Author: Janice Horne

Description: Use this activity as a way to revisit content. It works great after lunch on the second day of a multi-day training. Participants answer questions correctly and then roll two dice.

Objective: Revisit information to improve retention

Audience: Any training audience

Time: 20 minutes

Group Size: Under 20. No more than four table groups.

Materials: Trainer-prepared quiz questions, one set of ace through nine playing cards (or 3"x5" cards with the numbers 1 through 9 written on them) for each table, two large foam dice

Process: This activity is reminiscent of a board game with many names such as Canoga, High Roller, Countdown or Shut the Box. In this version, participants answer questions correctly and then roll two dice. They must add the values on the dice together and then turn over one combination of cards that equals the total on both dice. The object is to be the first team to turn over all of the cards. Note: if the Ace or 1 card is the only card not turned over, they can not win because they must add both dice together.

1. Invite the participants to gather around a table that has been set with the cards (one set of 1-9 for each group).

2. Inform participants that they will each have a chance to answer a question. When the trainer asks the question, the participant may confer with the team before answering.

3. If the question is answered correctly, the participant rolls both dice and his or her team can choose which cards they want to turn over.

4. Then move to one of the participants on the next team and repeat. The team that turns over all of its cards first wins.

Variations:
1. Set a timer, and the team with the most cards turned over at the end of time wins.

2. Towards the end, give participants two rolls per correct answer.

3. Rather than you providing all the questions, have participants create questions in advance of the activity.

1 2 3 4 5 6 7 8 9

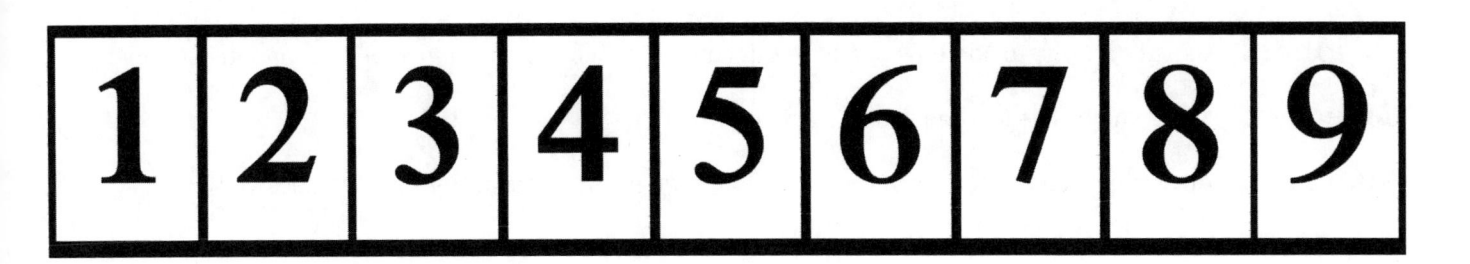

Here is what the initial set-up looks like.

Example of turning the cards: On a roll of nine, participants could turn any of the following combinations. This group chose to turn 2 and 7.

1 and 8

2 and 7

3 and 6

4 and 5

9

1, 2, 6

1, 3, 5

2, 3, 4

1 ✿ 3 4 5 6 ✿ 8 9

Super Closers, Openers, Revisiters, Energizers, Volume 3

☐ ☐ ☐ UP AND AT 'EM

Author: Karen Carlson

Description: Use this activity to add energy and revisit content especially after lunch or after an intense topic.

Objective: Share knowledge learned in a fun, active setting.

Audience: Any training audience; you will need to adapt it if participants have mobility issues.

Time: 5 minutes

Group Size: Any size

Materials: Pre-printed question/activity cards

Process:
1. Have each participant pair up with someone at another table, preferably someone they haven't had a chance to interact with yet, and then find a space in the room together.
2. Provide each pair with several question/activity cards. While standing up, one person reads the card aloud. The partner answers the question while performing the activity listed on the card.

Up & At 'Em!	Up & At 'Em!
Activity: Sit down and stand up while answering the question. *Question:*	*Activity:* Flap your arms like a chicken while answering the question. *Question:*
Up & At 'Em!	Up & At 'Em!
Activity: Lift your left arm out to the side while answering the question. *Question:*	*Activity:* Lift your right arm out to the side while answering the question. *Question:*
Up & At 'Em!	Up & At 'Em!
Activity: Clap your hands behind your back while answering the question. *Question:*	*Activity:* Balance on your left foot while answering the question. *Question:*

Up & At 'Em! *Activity:* Balance on your right foot while answering the question. *Question:*	**Up & At 'Em!** *Activity:* March in place while answering the question. *Question:*
Up & At 'Em! *Activity:* Stand on your tip-toes while answering the question. *Question:*	**Up & At 'Em!** *Activity:* Pat your head and rub your stomach while answering the question. *Question:*
Up & At 'Em! *Activity:* Do arm circles while answering the question. *Question:*	**Up & At 'Em!** *Activity:* Lift your left leg while answering the question. *Question:*
Up & At 'Em! *Activity:* Lift your right leg while answering the question. *Question:*	**Up & At 'Em!** *Activity:* Do bicep curls while answering the question. *Question:*
Up & At 'Em! *Activity:* *Question:*	**Up & At 'Em!** *Activity:* *Question:*

Debrief: Have the group share any questions they struggled with or found especially thought-provoking. Discuss possible answers as a group.

Super Closers, Openers, Revisiters, Energizers, Volume 3

SCORE III: SUPER CLOSERS, OPENERS, REVISITERS AND ENERGIZERS

ENERGIZERS — MENTAL STIMULATORS and PHYSICAL ACTIVATORS

Great presentations and training sessions keep participants energized through the use of effective presentation methods as well as mental stimulators and physical energizers. This section of the SCORE! book offers a variety of energizers to keep participants active and engaged.

Energizers are useful throughout a session, and probably are most useful during these times: after lunch, after a break, when the room temperature is too warm, and during the middle of a long content presentation.

This section contains both mental stimulators and physical energizers. The mental stimulators create "mental sparks" that stimulate the brain and keep participants ready to learn. This set of activities includes memory stimulators, trivia tests, quizzes and thought provokers. Mental stimulators are useful after breaks or after lunch as a way to re-focus the group on the topic at hand or to stimulate the brain and get participants back into a learning mood.

Make sure to use these types of activities purposefully and strategically. The audience should have a sense of why you are doing them. Using simple statements such as "Okay, let's get our minds focused back on the learning process by starting with this simple quiz," or "Let's wake up our brains this afternoon by examining this trivia test" will help participants understand why you are doing the activity or exercise.

When used correctly, mental stimulators literally create energy in the group. You can see the physical energy increase through the mental stimulation.

The activities included here are easy to use. Copy them and hand them out to participants or read them to the group at appropriate times.

Physical Activators get the body moving. These activities are often childlike, competitive and fun. They range from simple stretching exercises to those that involve fairly sophisticated brain-body coordination. Some of these physical activators are also designed to be controlled stretch breaks; they involve some questions or activities that can be related to the session content, thus creating a double win – a stretch for the participants and a learning point to be communicated.

When used correctly, physical activators will get participants back into a learning mood with a refreshed body and a re-focused mind. Although many of these are not content-related, most participants will make the connection between the activity and the purpose for which it was intended – to help the learning process. Enjoy these physical activators and mental stimulators.

http://bit.ly/SCORE3Energizers

BACK TO BACK COUNTING ☐ ☐ ☐

Author: Becky Pluth

Description: Get people moving and brains engaging with a simple math competition.

Objective: Get people energized for more learning with a simple competition.

Audience: Any training, presentation or meeting audience

Time: 5 minutes

Group Size: Any size

Materials: A partner

Process:
1. Have participants get up and find a partner with whom they should stand back to back.

2. Share that you will count to three and say, "Go!" Partners will then jump and face each other holding up any number of fingers from 1-10. The first person to count the total number of fingers up between both partners receives a point. For example, if partner A held up 4 fingers and partner B held up 8, the first person to shout out 12 would get the point.

3. Each pair will be doing this on their own with their own choice of numbers.

4. Have pairs repeat until you call time.

5. The partner with the most points wins the friendly wager.

6. Partners can give one another a high five or a hand shake and have a seat.

Variations: Have pairs do subtraction or challenge them with multiplication. I have yet to have a group successfully do the square root of their partner's number!

http://bit.ly/SCORE3BTB

Super Closers, Openers, Revisiters, Energizers, Volume 3

BOARD MEETING

Author: Marc Ratcliffe

Description: Oh, the joys of meetings! This activity aims at highlighting counter-productive behavior in meetings by introducing a fun mock meeting. It could be used in a variety of ways: as a warm-up exercise, a stereotype debunker or as a means to highlight some of the communication challenges in meetings.

Objective: Identify communication barriers that occur when conducting meetings

Audience: Any audience

Time: 45 minutes

Group Size: 8-15 people

Materials: One copy of the Board Meeting Game Card Template cut apart

Process:
1. Explain to the group that they are going to conduct a mock board meeting. Issue one game card to each person. Each person is to act out this role during the board meeting regardless of how they really feel.

2. Appoint a chairperson who needs to bring the meeting to order and instruct the group that this is a special board meeting to discuss the introduction of vending machines to the office lunchrooms. They are to discuss their preference for the type of vending machines (e.g. drinks, snacks, both, etc.) and a decision has to be reached in 15 minutes.

Debrief: Debrief this activity by getting the participants to identify some of the counter-productive behaviors exhibited and discuss strategies for overcoming these in meetings. As an extension, the trainer could ask the participants how they felt during the meeting (especially the chairman). It will be important to ensure that the participants recognize that they were playing an assigned role and the actions and behaviors were not real.

Variations: As a bit of fun, the trainer could get the participants to try to guess the identities of the other members at the end.

The Board Meeting - Game Card Template

1. THE CHAIRPERSON You are the chairman of the board, and your job is to bring the meeting to order and ensure the key issue is discussed.	2. THE COMPLAINER You complain about everything. Nothing is working for you.	3. DR. SMITH (from Lost in Space) You are the worrier of the group: "Oh the pain, the pain." You wonder what could go wrong.
4. THE AGGRESSOR You want everything your way. You will shout over others and try to intimidate them.	5. THE FIDGETER You find it difficult to stay still and play with everything - pens, paper, your hair, clothes, etc.	6. THE JOKER Everything is funny to you; it's "a crack a minute" time for you!
7. THE SHY TYPE You are reserved and don't say much. You might even withdraw yourself from some discussions.	8. THE DRINKER You need to be drinking something all the time. You get coffee or tea regularly.	9. THE PIG You are rude, often chauvinistic and mean. You try to offend as many people as you can!
10. THE FORMER CHAIRPERSON You were voted out recently and are still bitter. You want to make life tough for the new chairman.	11. THE HEALTH NUT You are against fatty foods and non-healthy food being introduced. In fact you would rather call this a "lentil-ing" rather than a "meat-ing."	12. THE DISTRACTOR You think meetings are boring and try to take the group off track as much as possible.
13. THE DEVIL'S ADVOCATE You are always looking at the other side thinking, "What if?"	14. THE STUD/BABE You are a Latin god/goddess. You are beautiful, and you know it. You speak English with a Spanish accent.	15. THE MEDIATOR You are a concerned and sensitive kind of person. You are always looking to attain a win-win situation.

Super Closers, Openers, Revisiters, Energizers, Volume 3

CROSS LATERAL STRETCH ☐ ☐ ☐

Author: Becky Pluth

Description: Using both sides of the brain and the body is a great way to start up after a break or lunch. When it is a nice day and the afternoon feels a bit sluggish, participants love heading outdoors for some fresh air and a stretch break. No materials are required; just bring yourself!

Objective: Quickly refocus a group and get people standing up. Because you are using movements that are cross lateral (where arms or legs cross over the body), it stimulates and engages both sides of the brain for a mental and physical pick-me-up. These movements are designed to improve attention and ability to learn new information.

Audience: Any training audience

Time: 5 minutes

Group Size: Unlimited

Materials: A partner

Process:
1. Have participants stand and get some space around them.
2. Share that you will be modeling a cross lateral movement that they are to mirror.
3. Examples of movements:
   A. Right hand to the left shoulder
   B. Right hand to left knee
   C. Hold right foot with left hand while hopping on left foot
   D. Left hand to right ear
   E. Left elbow to right knee

Variations:
1. Have participants make up the movements.
2. Partner up and mirror your partner's movements.

http://bit.ly/SCORE3CLS

FANCY FEET

Author: Becky Pluth

Description: This is a great exercise to use when a group needs a mental stimulator and a physical activator. I usually use this in the afternoon because it gets people dancing without them even knowing it!

Objective: Quickly refocus a group and get people standing up. It works not only as a mental stimulator but a physical one as well.

Audience: Any training audience

Time: 5 minutes

Group Size: Unlimited

Materials: A partner

Process:
1. Have participants get up and find a partner
2. Partners stand facing one another.
3. Choose one partner to be A and one to be B.
4. A's go first by moving their feet while the B's must mirror their partner's fancy footwork.
5. After a few seconds, see how they are doing and call time. Then have partners switch roles with B's leading the "dance."

http://bit.ly/SCORE3FF

GETTING TO THE POINT ☐ ☐ ☐

Author: Becky Pluth

Description: Quickly get people energized physically and mentally. This could also be used as an opener if you ask participants to name one concept from the session on which they look forward to being challenged.

Objective: Quickly refocus a group and get people standing up. It works not only as a mental stimulator but a physical one as well.

Audience: Any training audience

Time: 3 minutes

Group Size: Unlimited

Materials: A partner

Process:
1. Ask the group if they are ready for a challenge! Have them get up and find a partner. One of them will be an A while the other a B. Pause while they stand and find a partner and select who is A and B.
2. Have all of the B's raise their hands and share they will go first while the A's will be doing the pointing.
3. Say, "B's, place your arms straight out in front of you palms down.
4. Cross your right arm over your left to form an X.
5. Keeping your arms crossed, turn your palms toward one another and clasp them together with fingers interlacing. The hands are now clasped backwards from how they usually clasp.
6. With hands still clasped (thumbs are facing the floor), bring your thumbs up toward your body and push hands through the opening by holding them close to your body.
7. A's, without touching your partner's finger, point at one of the 10 fingers. B's will need to lift up the finger being pointed at. A's will point several different times."
8. After a few attempts and laughter, call time and have partners swap positions with A's clasping their hands and B's doing the pointing.

Variations:
1. Instead of calling them A's and B's, do something fun or related to content. One partner could be Batman and the other Robin or Apple and Orange.
2. This could also become a contest. Put pairs into teams and see how many correct finger lifts they get in 30 seconds or have A's compete against B's for correct finger lifts. This is great for competitive groups like sales teams.

Super Closers, Openers, Revisiters, Energizers, Volume 3

☐ ☐ ☐   GREAT GENERATIONAL TRUTHS

Author: Rich Meiss

Description: Share these fun, generational "truths" to add some humor to your presentation.

Objective: Get participants nodding in agreement by sharing these sayings.

Audience: Any training, presentation or meeting audience

Time: 2 minutes

Group Size: Any size

Materials: PowerPoint slides or a flip chart pad with the sayings on them

Process: Put these sayings on PowerPoint slides and share them before or during a seminar, presentation or meeting to add some humor. These would be especially good for any type of generations training or any topic related to family, life balance, etc.

Great Truths that Little Children Have Learned:

- No matter how hard you try, you can't baptize cats.
- When your mom is mad at your dad, don't let her brush your hair.
- If your sister hits you, don't hit back. (They always catch the second person.)
- Never ask your 3-year-old brother to hold a tomato.
- Don't sneeze when someone is cutting your hair.
- You can't hide broccoli in a glass of milk.
- The best place to be when you're sad is Grandpa's lap.

Great Truths that Adults Have Learned:

- Raising teenagers is like nailing Jell-O to a tree.
- Wrinkles don't hurt.
- Families are like fudge – mostly sweet, but with a few nuts.
- Today's mighty oak is just yesterday's nut that held its ground.
- Laughing is good exercise. It's like jogging on the inside.
- Middle age is when you choose your cereal for the fiber, not the toy.

Great Truths about Growing Old

- Growing up is mandatory; growing old is optional.
- Forget the health food. You need all the preservatives you can get.
- When you fall down, you wonder what else you can do while you're down there.
- You know you're growing old when you get the same sensation from a rocking chair you once got from a roller coaster.
- It's frustrating when you know all the answers but nobody bothers to ask you the questions.
- Time may be a great healer, but it's a lousy beautician.
- Wisdom comes with age, but sometimes age comes all by itself.

Share these statements with someone who needs a laugh!

HOW YOU DOIN'?

Author: Scott Enebo

Description: This is an activity that encourages people to get to know each other's names while also infusing the class with energy and competition.

Objective: To encourage retention of names and to create an atmosphere of friendly competition while energizing an audience

Audience: Any training audience

Time: 5-15 minutes

Group Size: 10-100 people (with room to move)

Materials: Bed sheet or blanket

Process: This activity is most beneficial after people have had a chance to get to know the other names of the people in the room. It is helpful for people who know each other but not too well.

1. Begin by splitting the class roughly in half. Have each group get together and face the other group while leaving some space in the middle.

2. You will need a partner to facilitate this activity by holding up the bed sheet, but you may decide to switch this person out to let everyone get in on the fun.

3. Say, "In just a moment, we are going to raise a bed sheet and separate the two groups. While the sheet is raised, you and your group need to pick a person who will be the champion for your team. The champion from each team will then come and stand in front of the bed sheet facing the other team. We will then drop the bed sheet, and the two champions will race to see who can shout out the name of the other person first. We will then raise the bed sheet and repeat with a new person from each team. Keep track of your victories as there will be a prize for the winning team."

4. Clarify instructions before beginning.

5. Repeat for as many rounds as desired.

Debrief: While this may be treated as a simple energizer, here are some questions that you may choose to ask to help tie it into content.

- What was difficult about this activity? What was easy?
- How is this activity a reminder for us in our work?
- Is there any way that we could have created this game so that we were not two competing teams but rather one cohesive team?
- How are you going to tap into the resources in this room as opposed to treating others as the "competition"?

Variations: To use this as a closer, after the activity, ask everyone to meet someone from the other team and then share something they like to do outside of work as well as one key training takeaway.

http://bit.ly/SCORE3HYD

JOHN HANCOCK ☐ ☐ ☐

Author: Jaime Pylant

Description: Use this activity when participants seem tired and you need their minds alert.

Objective: Experience "practice makes perfect"

Audience: Any training audience

Time: 2-3 minutes

Group Size: Any size

Materials: Pen, one blank piece of paper per participant

Process:
1. Ask participants to find a blank piece of paper.
2. Have them draw a straight line in the middle from top to bottom.
3. On the left side, sign your complete name as many times as possible in 30 seconds using your left hand.
4. After 30 seconds, ask the participants to stop and switch the pen to the right hand.
5. Then say, "Using the right side of the page, sign your complete name as many times as possible in 30 seconds. You must use your right hand."
6. Give participants 30 seconds, and then stop them.
7. Ask them to count up the totals from each column.

Debrief: What does this activity teach us? Practice makes perfect, regardless of which column you consider your best work. You weren't a natural when you learned to sign your name, but years of practice has made it become natural to you. The same will happen with this content, if you just practice and use it. If both are equally beautiful, congratulations! Maybe you're ambidextrous. So was Gerald Ford.

Variations: Instead of signing their name, have participants write the name of a system or topic they are learning about.

* Note: The New York Times reports roughly 10 percent of the population is left handed. *"On the Left Hand, There Are No Easy Answers"* – Klass, March 6, 2011.

NEED CAFFEINE?

Author: Adrianne Roggenbuck

Description: This is an energizer to use when the group needs a shot of energy. It is especially effective in the morning.

Objective: To energize the group in an engaging way

Audience: Any training audience

Time: 7-10 minutes

Group Size: Any size, but will work best if the group is divided into smaller groups of 4-6 people

Materials: A PowerPoint slide or poster with the Top Ten List on it, timer

Process:
1. Ask the group if they are feeling the need for some caffeine to perk them up.
2. Divide the large group into smaller teams of 4-6 people.
3. Challenge the teams to create a list of the top 10 countries that produce coffee.
4. Put on a timer for 2½ minutes.
5. Share the top 10 list and award one point for each country they have on their list that is also on the master list. Award two points if the country is in the same numbered slot as the master list.
6. Teams total their points to determine the winning team.

Debrief: Prizes may be awarded to the winning team. Tell them this energizer was as good as a caffeine fix to wake them up and probably healthier for them.

The Top Ten coffee-producing countries:

1. Brazil
2. Vietnam
3. Colombia
4. Indonesia
5. Peru
6. Ethiopia
7. Mexico
8. India
9. Guatemala
10. Uganda

Taken from the *Top Ten of Everything 2012*, by Caroline Ash and Alexander Ash, Sterling Publishing, Sterling, NY.

☐ ☐ ☐ SNIGLETS

Author: Rich Meiss

Description: Use this fun exercise as a way to stimulate the brain and have some fun.

Objective: Have participants engage their brains by using their creativity.

Audience: Any training, presentation or meeting audience

Time: 5-10 minutes

Group Size: Any size

Materials: A copy of the exercise per person, a writing instrument

Process: Sniglets are words that don't appear in a dictionary but should. Match the sniglet (on the left on the next page) to its definition on the right by drawing a line.

Variation: A fun variation on this exercise is to have the participants create their own sniglets after completing the sniglets exercise. These may be based on the class content for the training session or meeting or based on something in their own area of expertise.

Sniglets

Sniglets are words that don't appear in a dictionary but should. Match the sniglet (on the left) to its definition on the right by drawing a line.

1. Accordionated (ah kor' de on ay tid)	A. The act of trying to control a released bowling ball by twisting one's body in the direction one wants the ball to go.
2. Aquadextrous (aqua dex trous)	B. To accelerate or decelerate rapidly in an attempt to remove a clinging insect from a car's windshield.
3. Arachnidiot (ar ak ni' di ot)	C. Being able to drive and refold a road map at the same time.
4. Bowlikinetics (boh lih kih neh' tiks)	D. A person who always pushes on a door marked "pull" or vice versa.
5. Bozone (bo zone)	E. Possessing the ability to turn the bathtub faucet on and off with your toes.
6. Bugpedal (bug' ped uhl)	F. A person who wanders into an "invisible" spider web and begins gyrating and flailing about wildly.
7. Caffidget (ka fij' it)	G. Gangly people sitting in front of you at the movies who, no matter what direction you lean, lean the same way.
8. Doork (dwark)	H. The person in the express lane of the grocery store with more than 10 items in the cart.
9. Eiffelites (eye' ful eyetz)	I. That ever changing address in memory which always causes programs to blow up.
10. Exaspirin (eks as' sprin)	J. To break up a Styrofoam coffee cup into several hundred pieces after consuming its contents.
11. Expresshole (eks press hole)	K. The substance surrounding stupid people that stops bright ideas from penetrating.
12. Flammabyte (flamm a byte)	L. Any bottle of pain reliever with an impossible-to-remove cotton wad at the top.

*Permission is granted by the authors for book purchasers to copy this page for seminars and meetings.

SNIGLETS

Sniglets Answers

1. Accordionated (ah kor' de on ay tid): Adjective. Being able to drive and refold a road map at the same time.
2. Aquadextrous (aqua dex trous): Adjective. Possessing the ability to turn the bathtub faucet on and off with your toes.
3. Arachnidiot (ar ak ni' di ot): Noun. A person, who, having wandered into an "invisible" spider web, begins gyrating and flailing about wildly.
4. Bowlikinetics (boh lih kih neh' tiks): Noun. The act of trying to control a released bowling ball by twisting one's body in the direction one wants the ball to go.
5. Bozone (bo zone): Noun. The substance surrounding stupid people that stops bright ideas from penetrating.
6. Bugpedal (bug' ped uhl): Verb. To accelerate or decelerate rapidly in an attempt to remove a clinging insect from a car's windshield.
7. Caffidget (ka fij' it): Verb. To break up a Styrofoam coffee cup into several hundred pieces after consuming its contents.
8. Doork (dwark): Noun. A person who always pushes on a door marked "pull" or vice versa.
9. Eiffelites (eye' ful eyetz): Noun. Gangly people sitting in front of you at the movies who, no matter what direction you lean, lean the same way.
10. Exaspirin (eks as' sprin): Noun. Any bottle of pain reliever with an impossible-to-remove cotton wad at the top.
11. Expresshole (eks press hole): Noun. The person in the express lane of the grocery store with more than 10 items in the cart.
12. Flammabyte (flamm a byte): Noun. That ever changing address in memory which always causes programs to blow up.

STATE LAND MAMMALS

Author: Rich Meiss

Description: Have participants identify the state mammal from different states.

Objective: Utilize an interesting trivia exercise to create teamwork.

Audience: Any training audience

Time: 10 minutes

Group Size: Any size

Materials: Copies of the exercise, perhaps a small prize such as candy for the winning table

Process: Make copies of the following exercise and distribute to each participant. Have them make their best guesses as to the answers.

Variations: Have participants work together in small groups to complete the exercise. For some added energy, have a small prize for the group that gets the most answers correct.

State Land Mammals

Below are listed the official state mammals of some of the United States. Match the states from the list on the bottom of the page to the correct mammal. Some animals will have more than one state matching to it, as noted below.

1. Eastern Grey Squirrel   _____
2. Ringtail   _____
3. Black Bear (3 states)   _____   _____   _____
4. American Buffalo   _____
5. Horse   _____
6. Armadillo   _____
7. Badger   _____
8. Mule   _____
9. Grizzly Bear (2 states)   _____   _____
10. Desert Bighorn Sheep   _____
11. White-tailed Deer (7 states)   _____   _____   _____
    _____   _____   _____   _____
12. Red Fox   _____
13. Buffalo   _____
14. Nokota Horse   _____
15. Rocky Mountain Elk   _____
16. Beaver   _____
17. Common Raccoon (2 states)   _____
18. Rocky Mountain Bighorn Sheep   _____
19. Coyote   _____

States Represented:

Alaska	Arizona	California	Colorado
Illinois	Kansas	Louisiana	Michigan
Mississippi	Missouri	Nebraska	Nevada
New Hampshire	New Jersey	New Mexico	New York
North Carolina	North Dakota	Ohio	Oklahoma
Pennsylvania	South Dakota	South Carolina	Tennessee
Texas	Utah	West Virginia	Wisconsin
Wyoming			

*Permission is granted by the authors for book purchasers to copy this page for seminars and meetings.

Super Closers, Openers, Revisiters, Energizers, Volume 3

State Land Mammals – Answers

1.	Eastern Grey Squirrel	North Carolina
2.	Ringtail	Arizona
3.	Black Bear (3 states)	Louisiana, New Mexico, West Virginia
4.	American Buffalo	Kansas
5.	Horse	New Jersey
6.	Armadillo	Texas
7.	Badger	Wisconsin
8.	Mule	Missouri
9.	Grizzly Bear (2 states)	California, Montana
10.	Desert Bighorn Sheep	Nevada
11.	White-tailed Deer (7 states)	Illinois, Michigan, Nebraska, New Hampshire, South Carolina, Pennsylvania, Ohio
12.	Red Fox	Mississippi
13.	Buffalo	Wyoming
14.	Nokota Horse	North Dakota
15.	Rocky Mountain Elk	Utah
16.	Beaver	New York
17.	Common Raccoon (2 states)	Oklahoma, Tennessee
18.	Rocky Mountain Bighorn Sheep	Colorado
19.	Coyote	South Dakota

SCORE! III

☐ ☐ ☐ SUPERHEROES

Author: Marc Ratcliffe

Description: This is a group storytelling activity which echoes back to the importance of a structure. It also promotes creativity and a sense of fun, which could be useful in balancing dry content. The basic premise here is that the superhero genre has a predictable structure. It usually centers on the following: A hero with a special power has to battle an archenemy (the villain) who has plotted a dastardly deed at an identified location. The villain usually has captured someone important as leverage, and the hero has to defeat the villain and save the person.

Objective: Demonstrate the elements of storytelling and the importance of structure

Audience: Beginning or intermediate knowledge level in relation to the content

Time: 30 minutes

Group Size: 8-30 participants

Materials: Prepared superhero cards

Process:
1. Set up the activity by creating eight sets of cards with the following headings: hero's first name, hero's last name, hero's special power, location, villain's first name, villain's last name, dastardly deed and person to save. The grid below has some sample options.

    Have a different color for each set of cards for easy navigation and pack up at the end of the activity.

2. Break the participants into groups of 3-5 people and ask them to collect one card from each category. Explain to the group that they are to create a superhero storyline based on the information on the cards. As the trainer, model a sample storyline to get things started. It shouldn't take more than 5 minutes for the groups to establish their basic storyline.

3. At the end, ask each group to present their superhero story and be prepared for a lot of laughter!

Hero's first name	Hero's last name	Hero's special power	Location
Captain	Fantastic	X-Ray vision	The park
Master	Magnificent	Can fly	The city hall
Princess	Awesome	Can create and throw fire	The beach
The Masked	Crusader	Telekinesis	An abandoned warehouse
Mister	Remarkable	Good grammar	The stadium
Lady	Wonder	Talks to animals	The airport
Villain's first name	**Villain's last name**	**Dastardly deed - Event**	**Person to save**
Doctor	Wasabi	Deadly virus	World leader
Colonel	Apocalypse	Insect invasion	The mayor
Maximum	Prejudice	Freeze ray	Hero's love interest
Ultimate	Destroyer	Towering inferno	Hero's family
Wicked	Evil	Control weather	Innocent bystander
Dame	Dastardly	Hidden bomb	Scientist

Debrief: When debriefing the activity, ask the audience about some of the similarities between their superhero story and planning in general. Listen for things like "defined structure," "clear start, middle and end" and "agreed solution." The trainer can continue to explain that once a structure has been determined, there can still be flexibility, creativity and fun as long as everyone gets to the same destination.

Variations:
1. This activity could be modified to speak directly to content. Rather than fictional characters and events, the trainer could ask participants to create a story based on real job roles, events and situations. For example, if the trainer was discussing the topic of workplace health and safety, the structure could involve "a workplace," "an area of risk," "persons affected by the risk" and "methods for reducing risk."

2. If superheroes are not your caper, then any genre could be used to spark the audience's creativity. This could include a romance novel summary, sitcom pitch or even Shakespearean-style tragedy.

TOP 10 ENERGY DRINK CONSUMERS

Author: Adrianne Roggenbuck

Description: This is an energizer to use when the group needs a shot of energy.

Objective: To energize the group in an engaging way.

Audience: Any training audience

Time: 10 minutes

Group Size: Any size, but will work best if the group is divided into smaller groups of 4-6 people

Materials: A PowerPoint slide or poster with the Top 10 list on it, timer

Process:
1. Divide the large group into smaller teams of 4-6 people.
2. Challenge the teams to create a list of the top 10 countries that consume sports and energy drinks.
3. Put on a timer for 2½ minutes.
4. After time is up, share the top 10 list and award one point for each country they have on their list that is also on the master list. Award two points if the country is in the same numbered slot as the master list.
5. Teams total their points to determine the winning team.

Debrief: Prizes may be awarded to the winning team.

The Top Ten countries which consume sports and energy drinks:

1) USA
2) Denmark
3) Japan
4) Ireland
5) Australia
6) UK
7) Taiwan (China)
8) Malaysia
9) New Zealand
10) Thailand

Taken from the *Top Ten of Everything 2012*, by Caroline Ash and Alexander Ash, Sterling Publishing, Sterling, NY.

☐ ☐ ☐ USUAL SUSPECTS

Author: Marc Ratcliffe

Description: The "Usual Suspects" is an analytical game that highlights the importance of having sufficient evidence to support a decision or judgment. It is also a useful activity for exploring (and exposing) myths and stereotypes. It presents the scenario of a jewelry heist with five possible suspects. The participants have to determine who they think is most likely to be involved based on information provided by the trainer. However, the information is released to participants in three stages thus blurring the edges of who may be involved.

Objective: Build awareness of stereotypes

Audience: Those with intermediate or advanced knowledge of the information being presented

Time: 30-45 minutes

Group Size: 8-30 people

Materials: The Usual Suspects information cards

Process:
1. Start by explaining to the participants that there has been a jewelry heist in a local shopping center. Before the lights went out, the following five people were in the store:

   - Security Guard
   - Former Sales Assistant
   - Retired Police Officer
   - 16-year-old Girl
   - David Hasselhoff

2. Inform the participants that they have to make a decision on who they think is most likely to be involved with the jewelry heist. Explain that there will be three rounds of information provided on each of the suspects. At the end of each round, the group has to confer and come up with their number one suspect. (The three rounds are denoted by the numbers 1, 2 and 3 on the Information cards.)

3. Once the final round has been completed, ask the participants to nominate who they think is responsible for the jewelry heist.

Debrief: The fact is that the evidence is only circumstantial and doesn't really lead to any of the suspects conclusively. Discuss with the participants why they made some of their decisions and extend by posing the question, "How did stereotypes affect our decision-making?" Finally, ask the participants to conclude with a discussion on how focusing on stereotypes could affect them in their job roles.

Variations: 1. As an extension, you could invite five of the audience members to act out the roles from the Usual Suspects Information Cards. Additionally, the audience could be allowed to ask additional questions of the suspects before coming up with a final decision.

2. Make everyone in the class a suspect with a different role and ask them to arrange themselves in a continuum from most likely to least likely. In the debrief, ask how they made their decisions.

Security Guard 1. No criminal history 2. Volunteers for Red Cross 3. Recently engaged	**Former Sales Assistant** 1. Still visits staff regularly 2. Boss accused this person of stealing while employed 3. Has a pocket full of diamonds
Retired Police Officer 1. Internal investigation on him for theft of seized items. 2. Has a gambling problem 3. Video surveillance places him in the store when items went missing	**16-year-old Girl** 1. Is skipping school 2. Has a drug problem 3. Video surveillance in shopping centre has evidence of shoplifting in Surfwear Shop next door
David Hasselhoff 1. Researching role in new TV show "Knight Watch" – episode "Jewelry Heist" 2. Lost money on the launch of latest CD – "Drop it like it's Hoff" 3. In-store CCTV has him holding the missing items 5 minutes prior to the heist	

Super Closers, Openers, Revisiters, Energizers, Volume 3

WHAT DO THEY STAND FOR?

Author: Rich Meiss

Description: Participants will guess what the abbreviations of well-known companies stand for.

Objective: Test the knowledge of participants on abbreviations for recognizable companies as a mental stimulator.

Audience: Any training or meeting audience

Time: 5-7 minutes

Group Size: Any size

Materials: Copies of the handout

Process: Hand out copies of the abbreviations sheet and have participants make their best guess as to the identity of each well-known company.

Variation: Have participants brainstorm any abbreviations or acronyms that are used in their own company but may not be known by everyone.

WHAT DO THEY STAND FOR?
Write the name of these recognizable companies on the line next to the abbreviation.

AFLAC _____

ALCOA _____

AMC Theatres _____

A T & T _____

CVS _____

FTD _____

FYE _____

GE _____

H & M _____

IBM _____

LG _____

Nabisco _____

3M _____

UPS _____

XEROX _____

* Permission is granted by the authors for book purchasers to copy this page for seminars and meetings.

Super Closers, Openers, Revisiters, Energizers, Volume 3

WHAT DO THEY STAND FOR?

Answers:

AFLAC	American Family Assurance Company
ALCOA	Aluminum Company of America
AMC Theatres	American Multi-Cinema
A T & T	American Telephone and Telegraph
CVS	Customer, Value and Service
FTD	Florists' Transworld Delivery
FYE	For Your Entertainment
GE	General Electric
H & M	Hennes and Mauritz
IBM	International Business Machines
LG	Lucky Goldstar Corporation originally; now Life's Good
Nabisco	National Biscuit Company
3M	Minnesota Mining and Manufacturing
UPS	United Parcel Service
XEROX	The acronym has no meaning

YOUR NAME IN LIGHTS! ☐ ☐ ☐

Your name can SHOW UP IN LIGHTS as a contributor of a closer, an opener, a revisiter or an energizer in our next publication.

Design and create any sort of opening and closing exercises.

Find new and creative ways to energize your participants and review or summarize content.

If we publish your idea in our next SCORE! book, you'll receive an updated copy with "YOUR NAME IN LIGHTS!" Copy this page and use the copy for your submission. Describe/draw your idea briefly but completely. Use the lines below and another sheet if necessary. Or send your submission by e-mail to rmeiss@bobpikegroup.com. We'll give you full credit for any ideas published.

_____
_____
_____
_____
_____
_____
_____

YOUR NAME: _____

COMPANY (IF APPLICABLE): _____

ADDRESS: _____

PHONE: _____ FAX: _____

E-MAIL: _____

Submit ideas to:

The Bob Pike Group

14530 Martin Drive

Eden Prairie, MN 55344

Fax: 952-829-0260

www.bobpikegroup.com

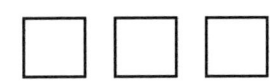

ABOUT THE AUTHORS

Becky Pike Pluth, M.Ed., CSP, MPCT
With more than 15 years as a training professional and two training industry best-selling books on the market, Becky Pike Pluth, The Bob Pike Group's president and CEO, doesn't rest on her laurels. As proof of her desire to continuously strive for "great," Becky was named one of *Training* magazine's Top 40 under 40 in 2012. She is the author of the award-winning *101 Movie Clips that Teach and Train* and *Webinars with WoW Factor*.

Rich Meiss, MBA, MPCT
Rich has been a participant-centered trainer with Bob Pike and other leading train-the-trainer organizations for more than 25 years. He has designed and taught numerous workshops to more than 65,000 trainers and leaders worldwide. His personal approach causes audiences to warm to him instantly. Most of his work is with repeat clients who continue to ask specifically for him. Rich is author or co-author of six books including *Coaching for Results* and *SCORE: Super Closers, Openers, Reviews and Energizers for Enhanced Results*.

Karen Carlson, MPCT
With more than 15 years of experience in learning and development, Karen has a proven track record of exceeding customer expectations and catering delivery and materials to the unique needs of each client. She includes adult learning methodology and recognizes the diverse learning styles of her audiences when designing materials.

Scott Enebo, M.A., MPCT
Scott Enebo is a strong advocate and model for creative and interactive training as he continues to see the impact it has on the participants experiencing the learning. Scott received his master's degree in intercultural relations with a focus on multicultural training. He also is trained in the ICA's Technology of Participation and enjoys conducting participatory strategic planning and action planning sessions.

Janice Horne, MPCT
Janice has a drive and enthusiasm for training and is motivated by the end result—an improved training experience by those who learn from her participants. Having thrived in retail, financial, and government organizations, Janice brings a wealth of skills to adult learning to help businesses focus on results-based action. Janice also is author of *The ABCs for Happy Living*.

Ayako Nakamura, MPCT
With more than two decades of training and development experience, Ayako is the founder of Dynamic Human Capital in Japan. She was awarded The Bob Pike Group Global Leadership Award in 2008 for her achievements in bringing Bob Pike's methods to Japan. Her client list includes Toshiba, SONY, Kanebo Cosmetics, Universal Studios – Japan, Boehringer-Ingelheim Japan, and Nomura Securities.

Bob Pike, CSP, CPAE, MPCT
Known as the "trainer's trainer," Bob Pike created and championed participant-centered training where instructors facilitate learning through the use of hands-on, interactive lessons, which research has shown as more effective than lecture. He has designed and delivered over 600 training programs of one day or longer and has authored or co-authored 30 books, including *The Creative Training Techniques Handbook*, which has sold more than 285,000 copies.

Jaime Pylant, MPCT
Jaime began training in 1999 as an instructor for the National Cheerleaders Association where he trained over 30,000 student athletes, coaches, and advisors and brings an enthusiasm and energy to learning that only a former cheerleader can! His training epiphany came after attending a Bob Pike Group Train-the-Trainer Boot Camp when he began focusng on developing participant-centered curriculum.

Marc Ratcliffe, M.Ed., MPCT
Marc founded MRWED Training and Assessment in Brisbane, Australia in 2000 which quickly became one of Australia's leading providers of trainer training. It has received numerous awards including the 2010 LearnX award for Best Workplace Trainer Training Program. Marc was named one of *Training* magazine's Top 10 young trainers in 2009. He is the author of *The Trainer's Toolkit* and the forthcoming book *The Trainer's Cook Book*.

Adrianne Roggenbuck, M.Ed., MPCT
Since joining The Bob Pike Group, Adrianne has championed Research-based Creative Teaching Strategies and Designing Lessons that SCORE, two workshops specifically for teachers. As a dynamic, memorable and inspirational trainer, Adrianne presents regularly at education conferences. She also is an adjunct instructor for graduate-level classes at Aurora University and Waubonsee Community College in Aurora, Ill.

Priscilla Shumway, M.Ed., MPCT
As a senior trainer for The Bob Pike Group, Priscilla brings a wealth of experience in adult education and technical training to her sessions and is a two-time recipient of the Pike's Peak Performer Award for content and facilitator performance. Priscilla has advanced studies in Accelerated Learning, Integrative Learning and Learning Styles. She also was a contributing author to *The Experts' Guide to the K-12 School Market*.

OTHER BOOKS BY THESE AUTHORS

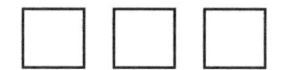

101 Movie Clips that Teach and Train

Using short clips from movies can relay learning points more dramatically and quickly than any lecture. Let this award-winning book jumpstart your creativity for lesson planning or training design by providing you with the perfect movie clip for over 100 topics including discrimination, leadership, team building, and sales. Each clip comes with cueing times, plot summary and scene context, and cogent discussion questions. All topics are cross-referenced so you can easily find the perfect clip for your teaching or training needs.

Webinars with WoW Factor

Death by webinar is rapidly replacing death by PowerPoint! Make your webinars effective and engaging!

Budget cuts and a business focus on everything "green" makes human resource training via webinars a really attractive option—IF you can do it effectively. Here is the resource you NEED for designing and delivering training that justifies your investment and gets the job done WELL.

Implementing these techniques and activities is guaranteed to better prepare you to involve your participants, make your training memorable, and ensure participant action planning.

These titles and more great resources for training effectively are available from The Bob Pike Group at www.BobPikeGroup.com/shop-products or by calling (952) 829-2658 or (800) 383-9210.

☐ ☐ ☐ OTHER BOOKS BY THESE AUTHORS

SCORE! Volumes 1 and 2

Someone has wisely remarked, "If you took all the bored participants from presentations, training sessions and meetings and laid them end to end – THEY'D BE A LOT MORE COMFORTABLE!"

Well, the purpose of *SCORE!* is to give you – the presenter, trainer or facilitator – a lot of ideas so your participants don't have to lie down to be more comfortable – they'll be challenged and stimulated by your presentation!

These are cookbooks. You don't have to read every page and try every recipe. Use the table of contents to help you focus on what you're hungriest for right now.

These two books have 138 additional closers, openers, revisiters and energizers for you.

All these titles and more great resources for training effectively are available from The Bob Pike Group at www.BobPikeGroup.com/shop-products or by calling (952) 829-2658 or (800)-383-9210.